THE VIRGIN COCKTAIL GARDEN

THE VIRGIN
COCKTAIL GARDEN

REFRESHING MOCKTAILS AND BOTANICAL COCKTAILS
MADE FROM THE FINEST FRUITS AND HERBAL INFUSIONS

DAVID HURST

CONTENTS

Welcome to *The Virgin Cocktail Garden*. Maybe you love the buzz of a good old-fashioned cocktail party or want to impress your guests with a sophisticated alcohol-free drink over dinner. Regardless, the recipes within will help you rise to any occasion, whatever it is and whoever happens to be there.

Botanical tonics, tinctures, syrups and infusions have a long history of being used as restoratives or for medicinal aid, and what better way to bring this tradition into the present than to twist them into delicious mocktails that bring the garden to your glass? In addition to tasting magnificent, they are full of vitamins and natural health benefits which are described in many of the recipe introductions.

All the drinks in this book can be enjoyed at any time of the year, but the whole idea behind this botanically-inspired book is to let the beauty of nature speak for itself, and what better way to do that than by eating and drinking with the rhythm of the seasons? A juicy strawberry drink on a hot summer day? A restorative, warm spicy beverage in the chilly winter months? Perfect. Also, depending on where you live some ingredients may be difficult to access out of season.

An aromatic dash of spice here; a heady hint of floral there – it's incredible what you can create when you use fresh, natural ingredients. And now, I share these inspired recipes with you in the hopes of showing you just how much you can do with simple, beautiful ingredients, the right equipment and a little know-how.

ALCOHOL-FREE ENJOYMENT

The drinks in this book are, by default, alcohol-free, but many can be made alcoholic by following the 'Add a Twist' instructions at the end of the recipe. I've done this because so many people choose to abstain nowadays, whether for health reasons, athletic pursuits or because they'd simply like a break.

In my experience, creating well-balanced and tasty virgin cocktails has always taken far more ingenuity. Non-alcoholic drinks have nothing to hide behind, and must rely on the quality of their ingredients to make them shine. The number of people who have cheerfully reported that my alcohol-free drinks 'actually taste really good' has filled me with so much joy.

Cocktail books often categorize recipes by spirit, but this one is by ingredient. I want to show you how versatile ingredients can be, as well as make it easy for you to find a drink to satisfy your craving. Want a tangy and refreshing drink on a hot afternoon? The Citrus chapter is for you. The only chapter not organised in this way is Pitcher Party, which suggests several drinks that can be made in large batches.

Most recipes in this book serve one, but if a bowl, jug, carafe, or pitcher is mentioned, you have an ideal drink for a group. Other drinks that scale up are those that tell you to 'top with' as this generally means you can make a large quantity of the base, divide it between glasses, add ice and top up.

To get the most from this book, first read through the equipment needed and the glassware that is required; while you can start out with a few different types of glasses, and build up your collection over time, you really need to have all the right tools of the trade before you make any of the recipes.

As with any recipe, read through the method to ensure you have the time, ingredients, and equipment before you begin. Too many times I've thought how nice a dish sounds and started to make it before getting to the part that says 'chill for 6 hours'; not ideal when I'm expecting guests in an hour!

HOW TO COCKTAIL YOUR MOCKTAIL

Gin pairs well with apple, elderflower and other herbs; try it in the Bee's Knees Martini (see page 77) or an Elderflower Collins (see page 38).

White rum is sweet so reduce the sugar syrup in any drink you add it to; the mojitos (see pages 44 and 46), Lychee Daiquiri (see page 100) and Piña Colada (see page 92) are well-known white rum based cocktails.

Whiskies and bourbons are caramelly, so a chocolate or dairy drink would be a good match; add a shot in a Blueberry Muffin (see page 142), a Vanilla Maple Shake (see page 64) or a Choc Orange Spice (see page 148).

Vodka is colourless and tasteless, so it's easy to add to cocktails; the Cosmopolitan (see page 121), Woo Woo (see page 117) and C Breeze (see page 118) are all classic vodka cocktails. Flavoured vodkas speak for themselves: if it's a mango cocktail, simply add a measure of mango vodka.

Tequila is great with lime, so the Ginger & Peach Margarita (see page 55) and the Lime Sweet Station (see page 83) would be grateful recipients of a shot of the Latin American spirit.

1 FIRST THINGS FIRST

THE ART OF MIXOLOGY

What makes a great cocktail? Or should we first look at what makes a great drink? A vodka and orange, also known as a Screwdriver in the world of cocktails, would be served in a regular bar and charged at a price one would expect to pay for a spirit and mixer. The bartender pours the vodka into the glass then simply tops up with orange juice. The Screwdriver, on the other hand, although containing exactly the same ingredients, will be served in a striking glass, with plenty of ice, a straw, a stirrer and a slice of orange on the rim. And the bartender may have shaken up the ingredients to wake the drink up and create a nice, lively, foamy head. For this presentation and theatre, you'd expect to pay a premium. Seen another way, all he's done here is market the drink.

So how do you market your own virgin cocktails for your guests? Appeal to their senses. Admittedly, not every cocktail will smell amazing, as it may not contain herbs or fruits with strong enough aromas, but you can always make your creations look good and taste great. Many of them will have a comforting sound associated with them, whether it's the clinking of the ice against the glass or the fizzing of soda water; they may feel good to the touch, through the coldness of the drink or the shape of the glass.

However, before you even arrive at the stage of having drinks that delight the senses, you need to look to the preparation stages. The art of crafting a cocktail, with or without alcohol, is akin to building a house: you need your land (your equipment and ingredients), then the building blocks (what you are going to put into the drink) and your tools (your shaker tin and other cocktail bar accoutrements). The garnishes, stirrers and straws are the final touches – the soft furnishings, if you like. And just like building a house, you're best off sticking to the rules first and making your first few builds simple but effective. Once you're confident in your ability to mix and match – and present (or market) your drink – you can be a bit more adventurous and go 'off piste' with your own variations, different types of glassware and cool and gorgeous garnishes.

Learn how to make a few cocktails well, so that you know the whole procedure for three or four favourites. Once you're well versed in making these, you can be a bit more ambitious. Making a good cocktail well is always preferable to not quite getting an extravagant cocktail right. Just as a clean plate is the greatest compliment to a chef, so an empty glass is to a mixologist. Like any hobby, the main thing is to enjoy it. Hopefully, you'll learn something new while you're busy impressing your guests and enjoying the sheer variety of nature's flavours.

Try making variations on the cocktails you already know: a cocktail with strawberry in it should work equally well with raspberry or blueberry. Swap a garnish – it should reflect at least one of the ingredients in the drink you're making. Replace milk with cream in a dairy drink for true indulgence, or use sparkling water instead of a lemonade top if you want less sweetness. Two words: be bold! After all, what's the worst that can happen? A drink that doesn't quite taste right, but at least you know which flavour combination doesn't work. You can put that knowledge to work next time.

TOOLS OF THE TRADE

Cocktail Shaker
Professional bartenders use a tin and Boston glass, inverting the glass and placing into the top of the tin. Aesthetics is the main reason: you can see the liquid being shaken. However, if you are more comfortable with a three-piece shaker, with a base, lid and cap, go ahead and use it. The most important thing is to get the basic principles right and feel comfortable with whatever equipment you choose.

Jiggers and Measuring Spoons
A jigger, or thimble measure, usually comes in 20 and 50 millimetre sizes. Measuring spoons, plastic or metal, are ideal for smaller amounts. In time, and with practice, you should be able to measure without using either.

Muddler
Metal, plastic or wooden, small, medium or large, they all do the same job. Use one to bruise or mash a herb or fruit, and wash it right away so it does not get clogged with old fruit.

Bar Spoon
A long-handled metal spoon, usually 1 teaspoon in volume, with a metal disc at the top end which can be used for muddling.

Strainers
A tea strainer or mini sieve is useful for separating solids and liquids. Professionals use a Hawthorne strainer, a metal implement comprised of a disc with a handle, and a spring around the edge of one side; the spring enables the disc to slot into the top of your mixing glass and strain out ice, fruit and herbs.

Blender
Always add liquid first, then leaves, seeds, fruit, et cetera as it is kinder to the blades. Start on the slowest setting, then speed it up to purée the drink. Check if

the motor will withstand whole ice cubes; a less expensive brand will have no problem dealing with fruit but its blades will soon become blunted by ice. Worse, the machine will just give up completely. If opting for a less powerful model, use ready-crushed ice.

Ice Crusher

If your blender can't crush ice, look into buying a manual or electric ice crusher. A manual crusher should only be used when you need a small amount of crushed ice – it's hard work! Or there is always the rolling pin.

Pineapple Corer

A pineapple corer is a great piece of kitchen apparatus. It won't take up too much space and, although it has only one use, will serve you well. Not only will it enable you to get out a large amount of pineapple in one go, it also gives you a pineapple shell into which you can pour your drink.

Citrus Press

A manual press looks good and does the job, but is quite unwieldy. A better option, which takes up far less space and is much quicker, is an electric citrus juicer. Simply cut the fruit in half and hold down on the plastic mould and get the motor to do the work. An economical and essential piece of kit for the kitchen.

Juicer

A juicer extracts the liquid from a fruit or vegetable and leaves behind the pulp. Because the juicer gives you only the liquid contained in the ingredient(s) used, it packs more nutrients in less volume than you would get with a blender, which leaves the fibre behind. Some argue that consuming the fibre is good, aiding digestion and making you feel fuller. Juicer versus blender is really down to personal taste.

GLASSWARE

First impressions matter. The analogy I draw for the significance of glassware, is that of someone going to an interview. When serving a large number of drinks, make sure the glasses are all of the same type. You may wish to lay them out so they form a circle, square, or triangle, for example, or arrange them so they form a letter

Casablanca	Hurricane	Martini	Coupe
A robust, ribbed glass; looks and feels like a very substantial glass. Ideal for anything you need to muddle and/or give a good stir.	Large stemmed glass with a fluted bowl shape. The Hurricane cocktail was invented in New Orleans containing rum and various fruit juices that required a large glass.	The archetypal cocktail glass, stemmed with a v-shape drinking bowl. Usually fairly low-volume glasses, whose ingredients contain quite strong flavours.	A stemmed glass often used to serve Champagne.

or number; the latter options are particularly effective when preparing drinks for a special occasion. On the other hand, when serving a smaller number of people, say between three to six guests, you may want to serve your drinks in different styles of glassware.

Margarita

This instantly recognizable glass is often used for cocktails such as the zesty margarita. This is also the glass of choice for frozen daiquiris.

Sling

A stemmed glass. The sling came about when a new style of glass was wanted for the Singapore Sling. The generic "sling" cocktail is with sweet-and-sour with a fizzy top.

Highball

The regular straight tall glass found in most private homes and bars/restaurants/ hotels. Suitable for long drinks, mixed drinks, fruit juices, water, carbonated drinks, etcetera.

Old fashioned lowball

A short glass with a wide brim and a thick base.

INGREDIENTS

The 'Essentials' are just that – items I recommend you buy now and stock all the time. Anything you buy from the Essentials list is a good flavor investment as these ingredients appear frequently in the book, so it's worth it to re-stock whenever your supply gets low. 'Particulars' are ingredients that are particular to only one or two recipes and are therefore unlikely to be used very often. Many are either non-perishable or have a long shelf life so all you're doing is building up your armory of ingredients.

ESSENTIALS	PARTICULARS	FRESH	SUNDRIES
Apple Juice	Agave Syrup	Basil	Serving Tray
Club Soda	Chocolate Syrup	Cardamom	Sip-stirs
Coconut Milk	Goji Berry Juice	Cream	Stirrers
Cranberry Juice	Hazelnut Syrup	Crushed Ice	Straws
Elderflower	Melon Syrup	Cubed Ice	
Cordial	Orgeat	Lemons	
Ginger Beer		Limes	
Grapefruit Juice		Milk	
Honey		Mint	
Lemon Juice		Oranges	
Lemonade		Rosemary	
Lime Juice		Thyme	
Orange Juice		Vanilla Ice Cream	
Peach Cordial		Vanilla Pods	
Pineapple Juice			
Sparkling Water			
Sugar Syrup			
Tonic Water			

MIXING IT UP

It's good to familiarize yourself with the following mixology terms before beginning. Most bartenders, most of the time, will use either the shake or stir methods. I do the same. Building, blending and muddling are also covered here.

Shake and Pour
Shake all the components of the drink into a cocktail shaker, with ice, and pour everything into the glass.

Shake and Strain
Shake all the components of the drink into a cocktail shaker, with ice, and retain the ice in the shaker.

Stir and Strain
The ice goes into the glass, cocktail shaker or jug with the other ingredients and they are all gently stirred together, then poured into the glass, with the ice kept back. Do this when vigorous shaking will bruise the ingredients.

Build
This entails pouring all the ingredients into the glass, which will already have ice in it, one after the other. Stir the drink well before serving.

Muddle
Use a muddler to extract flavour, usually from a herb or fruit. When muddling, it's important to remember that you are coaxing the flavour out of the herb or fruit by bruising it rather than bashing it into tiny pieces. You always need a little liquid to enable the muddling process, but don't add too much – it will splash you and also drown your fruits or herbs.

WATER AND ICE

Water

Tap, mineral or spring? Distilled, purified or filtered? Only to a well-trained palate is there any difference, so use what you have. The only big 'no' is to use fizzy or sparkling when 'water' is all that's called for.

Ice

First or last? Depends on your preference. If the ice goes into your cocktail shaker or blender first, then the ingredients you add cool the moment they hit the ice. Some mixologists argue that because the ice melts a little and dilutes the drink, this makes it a slightly inferior final drink. If you have freezing/chilling space available, use it! Ever been to a restaurant where the freezer they use to store the ice is very large, and it makes your heart sing? If you see this, you know that the drink-maker serves cold drinks cold. Keep your shaker tin, bar spoon and strainer in the freezer, too.

The larger the cube, the more volume and therefore the more effective it will be. So if you have an ice-cube maker or ice cube trays which make small cubes, consider buying large ice cubes or trays. Ice not only improves a drink's taste; it also feels good, looks good and sounds good, too.

Most shaken recipes call for the drink to be strained over fresh ice. This is because the moment you hand it over, it goes into someone's warm hand who may be standing in a heated room or lounging poolside.

STORE CUPBOARD

Here are a few pointers as to what you should stock to enable you to make a few drinks when the urge hits you or when surprise guests show up at your doorstep. And the more recipes you make, the more confidence you'll gain in trying out your own flavour combinations. It's a win-win scenario.

A few words on store-bought versus homemade: you can press or squeeze fruits to make fresh juices. You can produce your own cordials. You can blend your own fruit purées. There is a world of difference in a cocktail made from freshly squeezed limes or store-bought lime juice. Experiment. You are the best judge of what you like. I'm all for homemade but I'm also realistic, and know you have more pressing priorities than crafting an entire cupboard full of homemade cordials.

Fruit Purées
Blend fruits, such as berries, by washing them first, then add to the blender, gradually adding water so you achieve a consistency that make them easy to add to the drinks you're making. You can freeze your homemade purées in sturdy freezer bags. Alternatively, good quality fruit purées are commercially available; most contain only 5 to 10 per cent sugar. They are definitely not in the same category as store-bought fruit syrups, which have very little fruit in them.

Fruit Juices
Many of the recipes in this book contain juices that can be used in various formats. Take orange juice, for example: you can buy an economy-concentrated juice or go up a level to a brand name; then you can move up another notch to

the freshly squeezed juice. Remember that store-bought fresh-squeezed juice has had to be transported many miles. To prolong its shelf life, it contains preservatives and other additives. The very best way of ensuring you have only the juice of the fruit – and nothing extra – is by squeezing it yourself.

Fruit Cordials

To make 1 litre of fruit cordial you'll need about 1 kilo of fruit (strawberry, raspberry, blackberry, gooseberry, redcurrants, blackcurrants or a combination of any number of these). Wash the fruit gently and put into a large pan with 500 grams of sugar, 500 millilitres of water and the juice of 2 fresh lemons. Bring all of the ingredients to the boil and simmer for half an hour. Prepare a muslin bag by tying it to something so you can pour in the just-cooled mixture and let it drip through. (I use an inexpensive plastic tripod to set up my muslin bag.) This process should take around ninety minutes, after which you pour your homemade cordial into sterilized jars or bottles, seal them, and store them in a cool place, where they will keep, unopened, two to three months. Once you've opened the bottle, store in the fridge and use within a week. Once you've done this the first time, the next is easy.

SYRUPS

You're about to embark on a journey from trainee cocktail bartender to master mixologist, I hope, so you might want to consider making your own flavored syrups. Some words of advice, however, before you start boiling, simmering, and cooling: homemade syrup will last around a month whereas the bought version will have a shelf life of around one to two years. It needs to be pointed out, too, that there is very little difference in cost between homemade and shop-bought.

Generally speaking, to make a syrup you need equal amounts of sugar and water, plus the flavouring, brought to the boil then to a simmer to coax the flavour out. Some syrups, and some palates for that matter, are more suited to a ratio of 2 to 1 in favour of water; obviously a syrup with less sugar in gets a tick in the 'healthy' box, but don't downgrade sweetness too much or it will become a detriment to the taste of the syrup. See below for a few recipes for some of the easier-to-make syrups.

Sugar Syrup
This can be bought easily but it's so quick, easy, and inexpensive to make that maybe it should be the first homemade ingredient in your kitchen.

Put the same ratio of cold water to granulated sugar in a heavy-based pan and bring to the boil. As soon as it starts to boil, turn down the heat and stir well with a wooden spoon; you'll see that the liquid is gradually becoming clear and syrupy as the water absorbs all the sugar. Take off the heat. Leave to cool, then pour into a sterilised bottle and store in the fridge. It will keep for a couple of months.

Stevia Syrup

Stevia is many times sweeter than sugar, so you can use less stevia syrup in recipes that call for sugar syrup. It can be bought in its natural leaf format as powder or as a liquid. It's calorie-free too.

Gingerbread Syrup

Put 300 grams of golden caster sugar, 200 millilitres of water and 1 tablespoon of ground ginger into a pan. Add a cinnamon stick and bring to a gentle boil. Simmer for 5 minutes until the sugar has dissolved. Leave to cool and then pour into a sterilised bottle. Store in the fridge.

Cinnamon Syrup

Put 480 millilitres of water and 4 cinnamon sticks into a small pan; bring to the boil, then simmer for 10 minutes. Remove the cinnamon sticks, bring the water back to the boil and add 345 grams of sugar until it has dissolved. Cool and then pour into a sterilised bottle. Store in the fridge.

Chocolate Syrup

Put 480 millilitres of water into a small pan with a pinch of cinnamon and 2 tablespoons of cocoa powder; bring to the boil, reduce the heat and simmer gently for 10 minutes. Bring back to the boil then add 115 grams of sugar until it has dissolved. Add an optional teaspoon of vanilla extract for interest. Cool and then pour into a sterilised bottle. Store in the fridge.

Strawberry Syrup

Put 200 millilitres hot water into a pan – don't boil it – and stir in 200 grams of sugar until dissolved; add 280 grams of strawberries, reduce the heat and simmer for 10 minutes or so, stirring as you go. The syrup will reduce and thicken, and the strawberries will turn mushy. Cool, then strain into bottles and refrigerate.

GARNISH AND GLITZ

Apart from glasses, you need a continuous stock of straws, sip-stirs and stirrers. You may still have plastic straws at home in a cupboard and want to use them, but do consider paper straws when buying new ones. If using plastic straws, they should ideally be the black bendy rather than the multi-coloured, striped ones found in fast food restaurants. The smaller, much thinner straws, or sip-stirs (also called frappe straws), are so called as you sip through them and stir the drink with them. They are usually used in drinks served in lowballs, old-fashioned glasses or martini glasses. (Longer ones simply fall out of the drink.)

As for stirrers and themed events, you can really have some fun here. I've had events in the past where I've used stirrers in the form of tennis racquets and golf clubs, giraffes and cats, hearts and flowers. Light-up ice cubes are lots of fun, too and add a 'wow' factor to an evening event. They are totally safe, and you only need one to light up a drink.

Lastly, you need different sizes and types of trays to serve from. Non-slip black catering trays will work well for holding a lot of glasses, but a small wooden or metal tray will suffice when you only have one or two drinks on offer. Think about going to a local market or second-hand shop and picking up some trays, which you can paint yourself in a rustic style or in bright summery colours. Very little outlay and just a bit of time will yield great results.

2 HERBS

ELDERFLOWER

BASIL

MINT & THYME

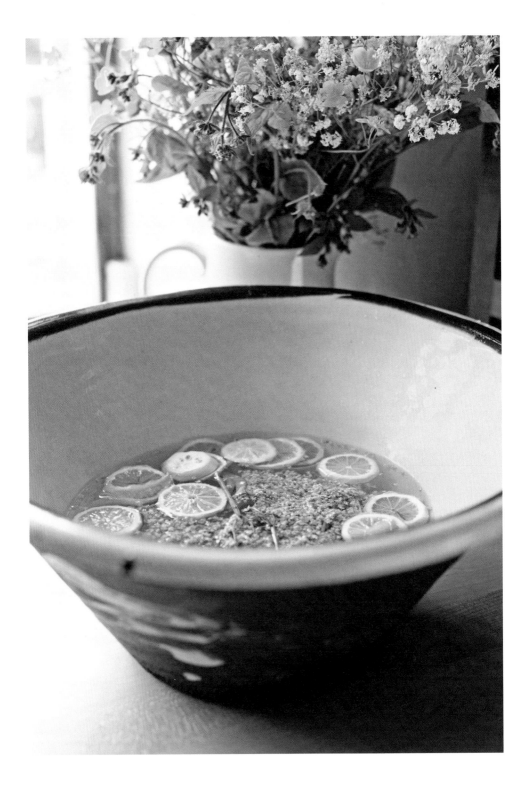

ELDERFLOWER FIZZ

INGREDIENTS

15 ml freshly squeezed
lemon juice
30 ml homemade
elderflower and lemon
syrup
150 ml red grape juice
Orange flavoured spring
water, to top up
Sprig of elderflower,
to garnish

ADD A TWIST

London Dry Gin plays
very nicely with the herbal
flavours in this recipe.

This delicious botanical drink uses an easy homemade syrup that is sure to impress. Elderflower, grape and lemon are a classic combination. This drink can easily be scaled up for a summer party.

METHOD

Fill a highball glass with ice and add lemon juice, syrup and grape juice. Stir to combine. Spritz the drink with orange-blossom scented water and garnish with a sprig of elderflower – I like to use a grape-coloured sweet William, but anything from your garden will look gorgeous.

ELDERFLOWER COLLINS

INGREDIENTS

1 tablespoon elderflower
  cordial
Juice of ½ lemon
10 ml vanilla extract
Sparkling water
Sugar syrup
Slice of lemon, to garnish

ADD A TWIST

I like to add gin to
anything with elderflower,
as it brings out some
lovely floral notes.

Elderflower has been used in traditional medicine all around the world and in many different cultures. Ideal for treating colds and flu, sinus infections and other respiratory problems, it can be taken orally as a rinse and/ or as a mouthwash. It can also be used as a diuretic and laxative. Despite its anti-bacterial and anti-viral properties, elderflower is also surprisingly sweet-smelling, a trait we showcase in this show-stopping drink. Its floral bouquet is a perfect match for the unmistakeable taste and aroma of vanilla. With a sweet and sour addition and sparkling water to add length and fizz, this is a delightful summer drink.

METHOD

Fill a highball glass a quarter full of ice cubes. Pour the elderflower cordial onto the ice along with the lemon juice and vanilla. Fill the glass two-thirds with sparkling water. Stir well. Add sugar syrup to taste. If needed, add more ice and stir again. Garnish with a slice of lemon on the rim of the glass.

THE ELDER STATESMAN

INGREDIENTS

1 cinnamon stick

3 cloves

5 coriander seeds

100 ml fresh pear juice

15 ml fresh lime juice

20 ml elderflower cordial

Club soda

Lime wedge, to garnish

ADD A TWIST

Replace the elderflower cordial with elderflower liqueur for a cocktail that is very low in alcohol.

This drink works because of how well the unexpected ingredients play off one another: the botanicals balance the elderflower; the pear brings the fruit factor into play; the lime points it up; and the soda gives the drink length and sparkle. Elderflowers themselves are wonderfully fragrant and the cordial they make has a grape-like aroma.

This drink requires advance preparation

.

METHOD

Place all of the spices into a cocktail shaker. Add the pear juice. Leave to infuse for half an hour. Remove the spices. Add the lime juice, the elderflower cordial and a handful of ice cubes. Shake well. Strain into an ice-filled highball glass. Top with club soda. Garnish with a lime wedge on the rim of the glass.

VICTORIAN GARDEN

20 ml elderflower cordial

10 ml fresh lime juice

75 ml freshly pressed
   apple juice

Sparkling water

Slice of apple and wedge of
   lime, to garnish

ADD A TWIST

For a sophisticated twist,
replace the sparkling
water with prosecco
or champagne.

This fresh, floral and fragrant drink is perfect
for a balmy summer evening outdoors.

Homemade cordials are a fabulous way to
serve guests a drink that bears your personal
flair. Yes, it takes a bit of time to prepare a
homemade cordial (see page 29), but once
bottled, it keeps for ages. To make a stand-out
drink, simply add sparkling water, tonic, soda
water or lemonade to a long glass filled with
ice and cordial.

METHOD

Add the elderflower cordial and the lime juice
to an ice-filled cocktail shaker. Pour in the apple
juice. Shake well. Strain into an ice-filled
highball glass. Top with sparkling water. Stir,
add a straw, and garnish with a slice of apple
and a lime wedge on the rim of the glass.

A BRUSH WITH BASIL

INGREDIENTS

6 fresh basil leaves
5 large strawberries
Dash of orange cordial
10 ml raspberry syrup
75 ml cranberry juice
Chopped strawberries,
  slice of lime and basil
  leaf, to garnish

ADD A TWIST

Gin or tequila would both
work well in this cocktail.

The slightly anise-like qualities of basil work well with the sweetness of fresh strawberries. For this drink, use regular sweet basil, as opposed to Thai or Greek, which are stronger and more peppery respectively. Basil is rich in vitamins A, C and K, as well as magnesium, potassium, iron and calcium.

METHOD

Muddle the basil leaves in the base of a cocktail shaker with the strawberries. Add the orange cordial, raspberry syrup and cranberry juice along with a good scoop of ice. Shake well. Fine-strain into a chilled highball glass. Drop in some chopped strawberry, place a slice of lime on the rim of the glass and top with a basil leaf.

SPICED PEAR MOJITO

INGREDIENTS

10 to 12 mint leaves
100 ml pear juice
3 lime wedges
10 ml sugar syrup
15 ml cinnamon syrup
  (see page 32)
25 ml sparkling water
Sprig of mint and wedges
  of lime, to garnish

ADD A TWIST

For a spicy version of the
traditional Cuban, add
white rum.

A delicious combination of herbs, fruit and spice that awakens various areas of your palate. If making your own cinnamon syrup, this is a drink you can truly call homemade. Extra points if the mint has been picked from your garden.

Feel free to vary the proportions to suit your taste. For more tartness, add another lime wedge. To sweeten, add more sugar syrup or for more spice, add more cinnamon syrup.

METHOD

This drink is made and served in the same glass. Place the mint leaves in a Casablanca glass and add a drop of pear juice, just enough to wet the leaves. Muddle for a few seconds. When you muddle, you are bruising the leaves just enough to coax out the flavour. Squeeze the lime wedges into the glass and drop them in, followed by the sugar syrup. Mint, sugar, and lime – the base of the Mojito. Add the cinnamon syrup and stir. Fill a glass two-thirds with crushed ice. Add the rest of the pear juice and sparkling water. Stir once more. Add two straws. Garnish with lime wedges and a sprig of mint.

MOJITO PASSION

INGREDIENTS

1 lime

2 passion fruit

1 green apple

1 cup cold filtered water

6 mint leaves

Crushed ice

Mint sprig, to garnish

ADD A TWIST

Add white rum for the perfect alcoholic version.

There is enough flavour in this virgin mojito that you won't miss the rum or sugar. Honest. You can swap the passion fruit for pomegranate seeds for a divine red mojito. This makes for another drink of starkly contrasting colours, as well as adding to the sensory impact: line up a few of these for a group of guests and they'll smell and see them as soon as they walk into the room.

METHOD

Cut the lime in half and squeeze the juice. Cut the passion fruits in half and scoop out the flesh. Cut the apple in half and discard the core and seeds. Place the lime juice, passion fruit and apple in a blender with half the water and whiz for a minute until smooth. Put the mint leaves in a Casblanca glass and muddle (use a muddler, or a wooden spoon if you don't have one.) Pour the juice over the mint. Add the ice and top with the rest of the water. Use the other end of your muddler or spoon to mix.

COCKTAIL THYME

INGREDIENTS

300 g granulated sugar

200 ml hot water

6 sprigs of lemon thyme

200 ml fresh lemon juice

3 wedges of fresh lemon

Soda water

3 lemon slices and sprig of lemon thyme, to garnish

ADD A TWIST

A lemon-flavoured gin is a great addition to give this drink some extra zing.

Thyme has a sweet, earthy taste, and gives off the most wonderful aroma, so much so that it is widely used in aromatherapy. There are various types of thyme available for culinary use: most frequently found in the kitchen is the regular 'common thyme', though lime, lemon and orange would be great variants to use here. Caraway thyme would give an aniseed-like flavour to this drink.

METHOD

First make the thyme-flavoured sugar syrup: dissolve the sugar into a pan of boiling water. Simmer until the sugar dissolves completely. Add the thyme and stand for 2 hours. Add the lemon juice. Stir well and strain into a small jug or container, then chill.

Now, make the drink: in a cocktail shaker, muddle two lemon wedges with a couple drops of the lemon-thyme syrup. Add the rest of the syrup and a handful of ice. Shake well. Strain into an ice-filled highball glass. Top with soda water. Garnish with lemon slices and a sprig of lemon thyme.

MINT & MELON MILK

INGREDIENTS

½ honeydew melon

125 ml coconut milk

Squeeze of fresh lime juice

4 leaves of fresh mint

1 teaspoon runny honey (or
   to taste)

Grated lime zest and sprig
   of mint, to garnish

ADD A TWIST

A single shot of coconut
rum adds a slightly
alcoholic twist.

Bartenders love mint. It grows in most conditions, usually annually, and quickly. And it's known the world over. Stick it into a garnish on the rim of a glass and your drink is transformed. Not only does it look great, it smells fresh, too. Use the leaf only as the stalks are bitter.

As with most of the recipes in the book it's best chill your ingredients in advance. However, so often it's a case of just deciding on the spur of the moment that you'd like something that's cool, healthy and tasty and uses up a certain ingredient, which may well be sitting in the fruit bowl or the store cupboard; in which case let the ice take care of it.

METHOD

Quarter the honeydew melon, remove the seeds, then reduce the quarters to wedges. Cut off the rind. Chop the melon flesh into chunks and blend with the rest of the ingredients and a handful of ice. Add honey to taste. Pour into a chilled highball glass, garnish with lime zest grated on the top of the drink and decorate with a sprig of mint.

3 SPICES

___

CARDAMOM

Coriander & Cardamom Tonic 52

Cardamom Martini 53

GINGER

Ginger & Peach Margarita 54

Earl Grey Lemon Mar-tea-ni 57

Ginger Zinger 58

Kooky Cookie 59

Spring Restorative 60

VANILLA

Vanilla Sky 62

Passion For Fashion 63

Vanilla Maple Shake 64

CORIANDER & CARDAMOM TONIC

INGREDIENTS

1 fresh vanilla pod

6 coriander seeds

3 black peppercorns

Sprig of rosemary

Strip of ginger

2 cardamom pods

½ cinnamon stick

2 centimeter-wide strip
    orange peel

2 centimeter-wide strip
    lemon peel

1 litre hot water

10 ml sugar syrup
    (optional)

20 ml fresh tomato juice

Tonic water

Wedge of lime and slice of
    lemon, to garnish

This fabulous-looking and tasting tonic drink will make anyone still nursing a plain old gin and tonic feel like they're settling for second best – and they are.

You need your own 'spicewater' for this, which can be produced in batches so you can introduce the liquid into other recipes in the book.

Make the spicewater a day in advance as it needs time for the flavours to infuse.

METHOD

Add all the spices and the peel to a heatproof Kilner jar. Add hot water and leave to steep for 24 hours. Shake gently to ensure the flavours are well integrated. Add sugar syrup to taste. Once you have the infusion to your liking, pour the liquid into another jar, filtering out all the ingredients using a sieve, muslin, tea strainer, coffee filter – whatever gets out all of the liquid with none of the residue. Add 50 millilitres of the spicewater to an ice-filled Casablance glass. Add the tomato juice. Top with tonic water. Garnish with a wedge of lime and a slice of lemon on the rim of the glass.

CARDAMOM MARTINI

INGREDIENTS

5 fresh cardamom pods
10 ml sugar syrup
25 ml still water, chilled
50 ml fresh pineapple juice
Wedge of pineapple and
   leaf, to garnish

ADD A TWIST

A pineapple- or orange-
flavoured vodka gives a
welcome fruity addition
to this cocktail.

This is a tried-and-trusted formula with those old bedfellows of fruit and spice.

Cardamom is usually used whole, as the seeds lose flavour when released from their case.

METHOD

Muddle the cardamom pods with the sugar syrup in the base of a cocktail shaker. Add the water and stir.

Add the pineapple juice and a handful of ice. Shake well. Fine-strain into a chilled highball glass. Garnish with the pineapple wedge on the rim of the glass and float a leaf on top of the drink.

GINGER & PEACH MARGARITA

INGREDIENTS

1 teaspoon grated ginger
1 drop of white peach purée
Juice of 1 large lime
15 ml orange cordial
Chilled water
1 teaspoon agave syrup
Slice of lime, to garnish
Salt for the glass rim,
 to serve

ADD A TWIST

Make this a twist on the classic margarita by adding tequila.

What's a margarita without alcohol? A puddle of lime juice? Quite the contrary. Replace tequila with agave and liqueur with orange cordial and the drink is reborn. Add some gingery spice and this version rivals any after-work special.

METHOD

Put the grated ginger and peach purée in a blender. Add the juice of a large lime, the orange cordial, chilled water, agave syrup and a handful of ice. Blend until the drink has the consistency of a slushie. Double strain into a coupette glass with a salt rim. Garnish with a lime slice on the rim.

EARL GREY LEMON MAR-TEA-NI

INGREDIENTS

Earl Grey tea
1 teaspoon finely
    chopped ginger
Juice from ½ lemon
10 ml sugar syrup
1 egg white
Grated lemon zest,
    to garnish

ADD A TWIST

Gin and ginger pair
together nicely in a
cocktail; you could also
add interest with rye
whisky.

The sharp, fresh taste of lemon and hot, spicy ginger are counterbalanced by the floral qualities of Earl Grey tea. The egg white gives the drink a rich and creamy texture and a frothy top. While complicated in its flavour profile, this drink is a cinch to make.

METHOD

Brew the tea. Let it cool with the bag still in the teapot; you want the tea to be strong and flavourful. Remove the teabag and pour the tea into a cocktail shaker. Add the ginger, lemon juice, sugar syrup, egg white and a handful of ice. Shake well. Double strain into a chilled martini glass. (Double strain to make sure no pieces of ginger end up in the finished drink.) Garnish with lemon zest grated on top of the drink.

GINGER ZINGER

INGREDIENTS

Thumb-sized piece of
  ginger
1 banana
100g kale
5 leaves of lettuce
Sprig of parsley (curly or
  flat leaf)
5 leaves of rainbow chard
1.8 ounces (¼ cup) frozen
  mixed berries
7 ounces still water
Sliced banana for garnish

A little ginger goes a long way – it can keep for up to a month in the fridge, making it a good item to always have in stock in the kitchen. An added bonus: a thumb-sized piece costs pennies. It's both long-lasting and cost-effective

I created this recipe while holidaying on the Isles of Scilly, where fresh fruit and vegetables are bought from 'honesty stalls'. (You simply leave your payment in drawers provided by the farmers.) Not only is this a wonderful way to shop, but it also leaves you in no doubt as to how fresh your salad ingredients are.

METHOD

Peel the ginger and banana. Blend all of the ingredients together. Pour into a highball glass. Garnish with slices of banana on the rim of the glass.

KOOKY COOKIE

INGREDIENTS

3 tablespoons caramel
    syrup

2 tablespoons heavy cream

2 tablespoons milk

1 tablespoon passion fruit
    syrup

1 tablespoon butterscotch
    syrup

Pinch of cinnamon powder
    and ½ teaspoon
    chocolate sprinkles for
    garnish

This sweet treat came about as a result of my two daughters asking if they could buy cookies for a train journey. I gave in and they both chose a different flavor. Having some time to kill on the trip, and keen to involve them in creating something fun, we came up with a flavour combination we thought would work well. When we arrived at our destination, we proceeded to mix them all up.

Here's the result, subsequently approved by grown-ups as well.

METHOD

Add all of the ingredients together into an ice-filled cocktail shaker. Shake well. Fine-strain into an ice-filled glass. Garnish with a pinch each of cinnamon powder and chocolate sprinkles.

SPRING RESTORATIVE

INGREDIENTS

1 green apple

3 celery stalks

½ cucumber

2.5 cm ginger

2 kale leaves

1 lemon

A crisp green apple combined with ginger makes this a refreshing and reviving drink that can be enjoyed at any time of the day. The addition of kale means that this drink delivers quite the nutritional punch. Kale is full of antioxidants and is an excellent source of vitamins A, K, C and B6.

METHOD

Cut the apple into quarters and remove the core and pips. Add to the juicer along with the celery. Peel the cucumber, cut into thin lengths and juice. Peel and add the ginger. Cut the stalks out of the kale and feed the leaves into the juicer. Peel the lemon, discarding any seeds and add to the juicer. Stir well and pour into a champagne saucer to serve.

VANILLA SKY

From sweet and sour to bitter and slightly nutty, this drink delivers a delicious and exciting range of tastes. The essence of vanilla has a lovely aroma and undertone, and helps make it a stand-out.

INGREDIENTS

10 ml sugar syrup
1 vanilla pod
75 ml freshly pressed
   pineapple juice
20 ml freshly squeezed pink
   grapefruit juice
20 ml coconut water
50 ml bitter lemon extract
Pineapple wedge and leaf,
   to garnish

METHOD

First, make vanilla-flavoured sugar syrup: put the sugar syrup into the pan. Split the vanilla pod down its centre. Add to the syrup and simmer for 15 minutes. Remove from the heat and allow to cool.

Fill a cocktail shaker with cubed ice. Add the just-cooled vanilla-flavoured sugar syrup along with the pineapple and grapefruit juices and coconut water. Shake well. Strain into a sling glass half full of crushed ice. Top with bitter lemon extract. Garnish with a pineapple wedge on the rim of the glass and float the pineapple leaf on the top of the drink.

ADD A TWIST

Dark rum is spicy and chocolatey, making it a nice pairing for this drink.

PASSION FOR FASHION

INGREDIENTS

75 ml hot water

60 g granulated sugar

1 fresh vanilla pod

2 passion fruit

Juice from ½ lime

25 ml passion fruit syrup

Slice of lime, to garnish

ADD A TWIST

Fruit-flavoured vodka, such as mango or coconut, would work nicely here.

This standout drink calls for a bit of infusion time, so be sure to plan ahead before you make it. The yellow, juicy pulp of the passion fruit is quite sour and contains gelatinous seeds, which add a dramatic touch to the final presentation.

METHOD

Combine the just-boiled water in a pan with the sugar and simmer until the sugar is fully dissolved. Add the vanilla pod and muddle for a few seconds. Leave the mixture to infuse for a couple of hours.

Add the cooled, sweet vanilla mixture to an ice-filled cocktail shaker. Halve the passion fruit and scrape out the flesh. Add to an ice-filled cocktail shaker along with the lime juice and the passion fruit syrup. Shake well. Strain into a chilled martini glass. Garnish with a slice of lime on the rim of the glass.

VANILLA MAPLE SHAKE

150 ml milk

2 teaspoons butter
   maple syrup

1 scoop vanilla ice cream

1 teaspoon almond extract

Finely grated dark
   chocolate, to garnish

ADD A TWIST

Whisky or bourbon would round out this drink well, adding a hint of caramel and spice.

Many of our cupboards at home contain a jar or bottle of maple syrup; it can come out at any time of the day. It's a great addition to breakfast waffles or porridge, lunchtime pancakes and after-dinner ice cream.

Experiment with the additional flavourings until you find your preferred shake.

METHOD

Blend all of the ingredients together along with a scoop of crushed ice. Pour into a highball glass. Garnish with some grated dark chocolate on the top of the drink.

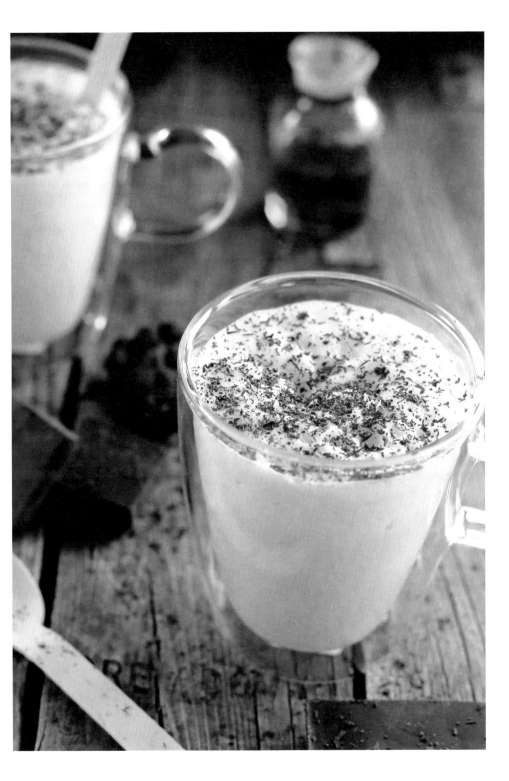

4 CITRUS

PAPA'S ORANGE FIZZ

INGREDIENTS

Juice from 5 large oranges
1 papaya
Sparkling water
Slice of orange, to garnish

ADD A TWIST

Try substituting the
sparkling water for a light,
dry prosecco for a twist on
the mimosa.

Two kinds of papayas are commonly grown:
one has sweet red or orange flesh and the other
has yellow flesh. In Australia these are called
'red papaya' and 'yellow pawpaw' respectively.
Another kind – picked green – is called a 'green
papaya', and is a staple in Thai cooking.

The colours of the drink and garnishes
together are the picture of freshness.

METHOD

Pour the juice from 5 large oranges into a
blender. Peel the papaya and remove its seeds.
Chop into chunks and add to blender. Blend
well. (You may need to add a little water to get
the right consistency – you are aiming for a
drink as opposed to a thick smoothie.) Pour
into a Casablanca glass. Top with sparkling
water. Stir well. Garnish with a slice of orange.

BREAKFAST BOOST

INGREDIENTS

150 ml freshly squeezed
blood orange juice
2 teaspoons strawberry jam
25 ml white grape juice
10 ml sugar syrup
Juice from wedge of lime
Ginger ale
Fresh strawberry and slice
of lime, to garnish

ADD A TWIST

Gin, vodka or tequila
would all work nicely in
this fruity drink.

A delicious blend of flavours. Use homemade jam to add fresh strawberry to this melange of different tastes.

Grape juices of all colours (red, white, purple and black) are high in antioxidant vitamin C, though the white variety has the most refreshing and crisp flavour.

METHOD

Squeeze the juice from the blood oranges. Put the jam into a cocktail shaker tin along with the grape juice. Stir well to dissolve the jam into the liquid. Add the sugar syrup, fresh lime and a good scoop of cubed ice. Shake well. Strain into an ice-filled highball glass. Top with ginger ale. (Replace the ginger ale with ginger beer for added kick.) Garnish with a whole strawberry and a slice of lime on the rim of the glass.

MAI TAI

75 ml orange juice
75 ml pineapple juice
Juice from 1 lime wedge
15 ml orgeat syrup
Grenadine
Pineapple wedge, slice of
    orange, and sprig of mint,
    to garnish

ADD A TWIST

Add a shot each of dark
and white rum, or for a
cocktail with a much
lower alcoholic content,
simply substitute orgeat
for Amaretto.

The Mai Tai is a versatile cocktail that can be
served long, short or straight up. The orgeat
– a type of almond syrup – adds, a distinctly
nutty flavour. Created by Trader Vic and
featured in his restaurant in Oakland,
California, the drink features both white and
dark rum. As rumor has it, the first lucky
recipient of the concoction exclaimed, 'Maita'i
– Roa ae', Tahitian for 'Out of this world! The
best!' This non-alcoholic version preserves the
drink's classic, almond-y tasting undertone and
is strained into an old-fashioned glass full of
crushed ice.

METHOD

Add the fresh orange and pineapple juices,
lime juice and the orgeat syrup to an ice-filled
cocktail shaker. Shake well. Strain into an
old-fashioned glass filled with crushed ice. For
a bit of colour, drizzle a touch of grenadine
over the top of the drink. Garnish extravagantly
with the pineapple wedge, slice of orange, and
a sprig of mint.

Homemade Lemonade
(see page 87)

TANGERINE DREAM

INGREDIENTS

5 large basil leaves

6 tangerine segments

15 ml sugar syrup

75 ml pink grapefruit juice

1 sprig of basil, to garnish

ADD A TWIST

Gin and citrus are lovely
together, and this
tangerine cocktail is
no exception.

The tangerine is sweeter and stronger than the
common orange. It's also easy to peel and can
be eaten 'on the go'. Its name originates from
the seaport of Tangier, Morocco, where the
fruits were first shipped.

Note: it's a good idea to muddle the tangerine
pieces first, then add the herbs to the mix and
be a bit less frenetic in your muddling action.
Gently does it.

METHOD

Muddle the basil leaves in the base of a cocktail
shaker along with the tangerine segments and
a drop of the sugar syrup. Add the pink
grapefruit juice, the rest of the sugar syrup and
a handful of ice. Shake well. Strain into an
ice-filled highball glass. Garnish with a sprig
of basil.

BEE'S KNEES MARTINI

INGREDIENTS

2 large oranges
½ lemon
15 ml peach flavoured
    spring water
10 ml runny honey
½ slice of lemon, to garnish

ADD A TWIST

A shot of Bombay
Sapphire gin will enhance
the botanical flavours in
this martini.

With fresh lemon and freshly squeezed orange juice, and as good a honey as you have in the cupboard, this is a delicious drink to serve at social occasions or simply as a great pick-me-up.

I serve this cocktail in a martini glass, which ideally should be well chilled. Take a large scoop of crushed ice and fill the whole glass, or place a scoopful of ice cubes in the glass and add a couple of tablespoons of chilled water. Discard the crushed ice or iced water just before putting the finished drink into the glass.

METHOD

Squeeze the juice of two large oranges into a cocktail shaker. Add the juice from half a lemon. Pour in the peach water and add the honey, taking care to stir it all together and ensure the honey doesn't remain stuck to the base of your shaker. Add the ice. Shake well. Strain into a chilled martini glass. Nectar!

CITRUS BELLINI

INGREDIENTS

15 ml fresh lemon juice
15 ml lime cordial
Sparkling water, chilled
    Lemonade (see page 87)
Slice of lemon, to garnish

ADD A TWIST

The substitution of sparkling water with prosecco is the obvious choice here, as the classic Bellini and its variations are always made with prosecco.

This is a citrus version of the classic Italian cocktail from the 1930s, so it has quite a zip and zing. Giuseppe Cipriani of Harry's Bar in Venice invented it, naming it after the 15th-century Venetian artist Giovanni Bellini.

This is a great example of a family of cocktails: a 'family' of well-known Italian artists' names have all been adopted as variants of the original Bellini. The Puccini has mandarin juice as its base and the Rossini uses strawberry purée, while the Tintoretto uses pomegranate juice.

The sparkling water may be enough on its own, especially if you like it drier. A few drops of lemonade provide added sweetness; it's barely noticeable but does add to the end result.

METHOD

Pour the fresh lemon juice and lime cordial into the bottom of a champagne flute. Top with sparkling water, leaving enough room for a finger of lemonade. Stir well but not too vigorously as otherwise the bubbles soon disappear and the drink loses its allure. Garnish with a slice of lemon on the rim of the glass.

SODA DAISY

INGREDIENTS

100 ml tonic water
10 ml grenadine
1 tablespoon lemon juice
100 ml soda water
Slice of lemon, to garnish
Strawberries, to garnish

ADD A TWIST

This drink tastes great with champagne in place of the tonic water – perfect for a summer celebration.

Quinine, citrus and pomegranate together provide an eclectic combination of tastes.

Grenadine is quite commonly used in the world of cocktails, gaining notoriety through the Shirley Temple, and is used to add both sweetness and colour. A spoonful swirling around the surface of a drink or inside the glass adds a theatrical effect.

METHOD

Pour the tonic water into an ice-filled highball glass. Add the grenadine and freshly squeezed lemon juice. Stir well. Add another few ice cubes, stir again, and top with the soda water. Leave room for another cube or two of ice as well as a wedge of fresh lemon.

ROSEMARY LEMON COOLER

INGREDIENTS

25 ml sugar syrup
2 sprigs of fresh rosemary
50 ml cranberry juice
Juice from lemon wedge
Soda water
Slice of lemon, to garnish

ADD A TWIST

Rosemary pairs well with gin, or to take it one step further, try switching out the soda water for prosecco. Be careful – it'll be strong.

Earthy rosemary, fresh lemon and dry cranberry form a terrific triumvirate of flavours. This infusion will need to be prepared well in advance of serving.

METHOD

Put the sugar syrup in a pan that's already on low heat. Add one sprig of rosemary; the warmth of the syrup will release the oils and tease the flavours out of the herb. Take the pan off the heat and let the rosemary steep for an hour. Remove the rosemary and chill. Add the syrup to an ice-filled cocktail shaker. Add the cranberry and lemon juices. Shake well. Strain into a Casablanca glass with large ice cubes in it. Top with soda water. Garnish with a slice of lemon on the rim of the glass and the other sprig of rosemary.

LIME SWEET STATION

INGREDIENTS

½ fresh lime

1 teaspoon honey

75 ml lemon-
    flavoured spring water

Lime wedge, to garnish

ADD A TWIST

Add a measure of
Cachaça, the Brazilian
national spirit, for a
great take on the well-
known Caipirinha.

I made up this drink after getting off a train at Liverpool's Lime Street Station; I didn't have an alcohol-free drink to offer guests arriving in an hour. The station's shops provided the flavoured water and honey. The venue's kitchen had a box of limes, and I crushed the ice with a rolling pin and tea towel.

This drink relies on the freshness of the lime and the quality of the honey. A warning: it takes a while to prepare. It's all about the stirring.

METHOD

Chop your half of lime into four, so you have four-eighths. Add two of the wedges to a sturdy old-fashioned or rocks glass. Muddle them well. Repeat with the remaining two pieces. Add the honey and a drop of the lemon water. Stir well. The honey will try its best to stick to the spoon, the lime, and the glass, but keep stirring and adding more lemon water until you have as much of it as possible mixed into the liquid. Add a scoop of crushed ice and stir again. Add another scoop of ice. Serve with two frappe straws and drop a wedge of lime into the drink.

SUMMER SUNSET

10 ml fresh grapefruit juice
15 ml pomegranate cordial
20 ml lemon juice
20 ml sugar syrup
½ litre of sparkling water
2 x ½ slice of pink
    grapefruit, to garnish

ADD A TWIST

Tequila and grapefruit are
a great duo, evidenced by
classic cocktails such as
the Paloma.

Pomegranate mixes perfectly with the citrus of the grapefruit, giving a delightfully effective sweet-and-sour combination. The health benefits of pomegranate are manifold: it's a good source of fibre and also contains vitamins A, C, and E, iron and other antioxidants, notably tannins.

This is a sharp and refreshing drink; the sharpness will be toned down to an extent by adding the sugar syrup, though adding too much detracts from the drink's characteristics. Best to add the sugar syrup to taste.

METHOD

Put the first four ingredients into an ice-filled cocktail shaker. Shake well. Strain into a highball glass half full of crushed ice. Top with another spoonful of crushed ice and the sparkling water. Garnish with half slices of grapefruit on the side of the glass.

GRAPEFRUIT BLAST

INGREDIENTS

100 ml grapefruit juice

100 ml orange juice

50 ml lemonade (see
   page 87)

Slice of orange, to garnish

ADD A TWIST

As with any citrus drink,
gin would be a welcome
addition, adding a
pleasant herbal note.

This is probably the simplest recipe in this book
and certainly the quickest to make.

Grapefruit comes in different shades of pink,
red and yellow and varies, too, in its acidity
and tartness, with some being slightly sweeter
than others. No matter the species or variety,
though, the grapefruit's sharp taste won't fail
to wake up your palate . . . or all of your senses
for that matter.

METHOD

Pour equal amounts of grapefruit and orange
juices in to an ice-filled highball glass. Top with
lemonade. Stir well to infuse the flavours. (You
may want to add a couple more cubes of ice
and give it another stir.) Garnish with a slice
of orange on the rim of the glass.

HOMEMADE LEMONADE

INGREDIENTS

8 large lemons

180 g granulated sugar

2 litres of water

Lemon wedge and sprig of
  rosemary (optional),
  to garnish

A great alternative to the commercially available versions, which bear little resemblance to 'the real McCoy' and are often high in sugar content. This recipe will make a large quantity and can be used wherever a recipe calls for the addition of lemonade.

METHOD

Clean the lemons by scrubbing them in warm water. Use a zester or peeler to take the zest off four of the lemons, making sure there is very little of the white pith left on them as this will make your finished lemonade taste quite bitter. Put the lemon zest into a large bowl and add the juice from all the lemons along with the sugar. There's no need to strain out the seeds at this stage. Stir well. Cool in the fridge for at least three hours. Once cooled, strain into a jug so there's no zest in your lemonade, or, if you prefer, pour it all in, zest and all. Pour into ice-filled highball glasses. Garnish with a lemon wedge dropped into each drink and a sprig of rosemary, if using.

5 TROPICAL

PINEAPPLE

Pineapple & Kale Boost   90

Tropical Storm   91

Piña Colada   92

Singapore Sling   94

Paradise Cooler   95

Caribbean Float   98

Tropical Sparkle   99

LYCHEE

Lychee Daiquiri   100

COCONUT

Bermudan Breeze   102

Beet It!   103

Tropical Cream   104

Cocoda   105

KIWI

Kiwi Kooler   106

AVOCADO & MANGO

Green Light   109

Rise and Shine 110

PINEAPPLE & KALE BOOST

INGREDIENTS

5 cm slice of pineapple
3 kale leaves
½ cucumber
½ vanilla pod
Pineapple wedge to garnish

Pineapple and kale may sound like an unusual combination but trust me, they work really well together. Zingy and fresh, with a hint of warmth coming from the vanilla. Replace the vanilla with fresh green chilli for added warmth and spice.

METHOD

Slice the skin off the pineapple, remove the core and cut the pineapple into cubes. Add to the juicer. Cut the stalks out of the kale and feed the leaves into the juicer. Peel the cucumber, add to the mixture and juice. Scrape out the seeds from the vanilla pod; you only need a little to flavour this so add a tiny amount of the seeds and taste as you go, adding more if you like. Add 1 tablespoon of water and then pour into an ice-filled highball glass and stir well before stirring.

TROPICAL STORM

INGREDIENTS

5 cm slice of pineapple

½ mango

¼ melon

250 ml coconut water

Pineapple wedge and leaf,
   to garnish

Kicking up a storm, pineapple, mango, melon and coconut are totally tropical bedfellows. In the case of a pineapple garnish, I always go for the wedge and leaf option, as the fruit is quite large and these parts of it won't be missed.

All the tropical fruits have high levels of vitamins A and C and manganese, which can be very useful in winter when other ripe fruits are scarce. If you buy the whole fruits, store any leftovers in the fridge and use as soon as possible; don't make up a large batch of juice because the vitamins and minerals oxidize quickly.

METHOD

Peel the pineapple, mango and melon and coarsely chop the fruit. Place in a blender, add the coconut water and whiz for one minute until smooth.

Pour into a chilled highball glass. Garnish with a pineapple wedge on the rim of the glass and float a leaf on the top of the drink.

PIÑA COLADA

1 small pineapple
100 ml milk
50 ml cream of coconut
Juice from 1 lime
1 pineapple shell,
    to garnish

ADD A TWIST

The most obvious addition here is white rum for an extra hit of tropical flavour.

The Piña Colada has been poured, shaken, muddled and blended by bartenders the world over; opt for the blended version as this drink is all about the pineapple. The lime simply emphasizes the flavour profile.

This drink leads the way in over-the-top garnishes and over-embellished presentation. Here, you use the pineapple shell to serve the drink, carving a small hole for the straw. The garnish becomes the glass!

METHOD

Cut off and set aside the leafy top of the pineapple; this top will become the lid. Scoop out the flesh of the pineapple. (There are special corers you can buy but a stout knife works well.) Blend the flesh along with milk, cream of coconut, lime juice and a scoop of ice. Pour into the hollowed-out pineapple shell. Make a hole in the lid wide enough to feed a straw through it. Place the lid on top of the shell. Enjoy.

SINGAPORE SLING

25 ml Morello cherry
   cordial
75 ml freshly squeezed
   pineapple juice
75 ml freshly squeezed
   orange juice
Juice of ½ lemon
Dash of Angostura bitters
Sparkling water
Pineapple wedge, cherry
   and orange slice,
   to garnish

ADD A TWIST

The addition of gin here
creates the classic
well-known cocktail.

What at first looks like an odd selection of ingredients becomes a harmonious balance. Call it the magic of mixology: I'm not a fan of some of the ingredients individually, yet I love the end product.

This cocktail was popularised at the Raffles Hotel in Singapore when the likes of Ernest Hemingway stayed there. Today, most Singapore Slings come pre-mixed and few bars serve them with the style and elegance of a few decades ago.

There are so many variants that the author of a 1948 book *The Fine Art of Mixing Drinks* states, 'Of all the recipes published for this drink I have never seen any two that were alike'. Here's my interpretation of a classic.

METHOD

Pour the Morello cherry cordial into an ice-filled cocktail shaker. Add the freshly squeezed pineapple and orange juices, the lemon juice and Angostura bitters. Shake well. Strain into an ice-filled highball glass. Top with sparkling water. Add a pineapple wedge and slice of orange on the rim of the glass, and top with a cherry.

PARADISE COOLER

INGREDIENTS

1 fresh guava
50 ml freshly pressed
   pineapple juice
50 ml freshly squeezed
   orange juice
Juice from ½ lime
10 ml grenadine
Pineapple leaves, to garnish

ADD A TWIST

An aged, dark rum would
add a spicy undertone to
the bright, fruity elements
in this beverage.

Guava has one of the highest concentrations
of antioxidants and is a rich source of fibre. A
guava a day keeps the doctor away!

METHOD

Peel the guava and remove its seeds. Put the
guava flesh into the blender along with the
fruit juices and lime juice. Add a good scoop
of crushed ice. Blend. Pour into an ice-filled
highball glass and drizzle grenadine over the
top to create a bleeding effect. Garnish with
pineapple leaves.

Tropical Sparkle
(see page 99)

CARIBBEAN FLOAT

INGREDIENTS

1 small pineapple

Large scoop vanilla
   ice cream

125 ml sparkling water

125 ml coconut milk

Pineapple leaves,
   to garnish

Fresh pineapple is a terrific fruit for dieters. It contains bromelain, a mixture of enzymes that helps digestion and breaks down fats and protein. Swap out the vanilla ice cream in this drink for a more low-calorie substitute and you've got a delicious treat for any 'cheat day'.

The hurricane glass is one you probably won't know by name but will certainly recognize from its distinctive shape. It's great to keep a few of these fabulous glasses on hand – they help transform any get-together into something, well, a bit more special. Guests love them.

If you do decide to go with ice cream, it's important that you use the very best you can get, as it will make a discernable difference.

METHOD

For this drink, you use the pineapple shell as the drink's glass. Carefully core and cut up the pineapple, leaving at least half of the pineapple shell intact. Place the pineapple flesh in blender along with the ice cream, water, milk and a scoop of ice. Blend well. Pour into the pineapple shell. Float the pineapple leaves on the drink.

TROPICAL SPARKLE

INGREDIENTS

100 ml pineapple juice

20 ml lemon juice

Juice from lime wedge

100 ml tonic water

Pineapple wedge and leaf,
   to garnish

ADD A TWIST

A shot of coconut rum is a great choice to pair with the pineapple flavour of this drink.

The pineapple, or 'piña' in Spanish and 'ananas' in Hispanic American countries, is versatile, with many health benefits. A 20 gram serving contains half the recommended daily intake of magnesium and vitamin C. It soothes coughs, sore throats and upset stomachs.

This is relatively simple to make – just add the ingredients and give it a good shake. The trick is to make sure the ingredients have been mixed thoroughly. I prefer to add ice to the shaker first so that the ingredients can make immediate contact with the ice and are chilled right away. Other drinkologists add ice as the last ingredient so as to avoid the possibility of dilution. The choice, of course, is yours, and will depend on your personal taste.

METHOD

Pour the pineapple and lemon juices into an ice-filled cocktail shaker. Squeeze in a little lime. Shake well. Strain into an ice-filled highball glass. Top with tonic water. Garnish with a pineapple wedge on the rim of the glass and float a leaf on the top of the drink.

LYCHEE DAIQUIRI

35 ml lychee juice
25 ml fresh lime juice
15 ml blackcurrant syrup
10 ml sugar syrup
½ slice of lime, to garnish

ADD A TWIST

This daiquiri loves to team with white or golden rum.

Freshly squeezed lime juice is a key ingredient in a daiquiri. In the mining town of Daiquiri, Cuba, crude rum was given to malaria victims. The taste was disguised by adding fruity, zesty lime juice and, so that the drink didn't taste so sharp, sweetening it with sugar. And thus the daiquiri was born. In turn, various fruit flavours were added, the most common being the Strawberry Daiquiri. I have taken a more exotic fruit – the blackcurrant – for added sweetness.

The daiquiri can be served in a variety of ways: straight up, short over ice or frozen. This is the martini glass version. The short version is served in an old-fashioned glass over ice cubes. The frozen version is blended with ice, but only give a short blast on the blender so shards of ice remain in the finished drink.

METHOD

Add all the ingredients to an ice-filled cocktail shaker. Shake well. Strain into a chilled, frosted martini glass. Garnish with a slice of lime on the rim of the glass.

BERMUDAN BREEZE

INGREDIENTS

½ small pineapple
150 ml coconut milk
Juice from lime wedge
125 ml ginger ale
Pineapple wedge and
   maraschino cherry,
   to garnish

ADD A TWIST

Add a measure of mango vodka for an added measure of alcoholic fruitiness.

The secret to this drink is ginger ale; it spices up the tropical flavour nicely. Ginger beer is a bit too spicy but, depending on your taste preference, you may want to give it a try, too. The coconut milk smoothes the concoction to perfection.

Note: coconut milk is quite different from coconut water; its juice is extracted by pressing the grated white coconut kernel. It has a high fat content (24 per cent); health-conscious individuals should consider using the light version. Today, both options are easy to find in supermarkets and online.

METHOD

Core and chop the pineapple and place in a blender along with the coconut milk, lime juice and a scoop of crushed ice. Blend well. Pour into a highball glass. Add the ginger ale and stir. Garnish with a pineapple wedge and a maraschino cherry on the rim of the glass.

BEET IT!

½ beet root

Handful of beet greens

125 ml coconut water

Juice of ½ lime

Grated lime zest, to garnish

For this recipe, I use the root of the beet and the greens of the plant. With vitamins A and K, beets boost the immune system and support healthy bones.

METHOD

Scrub the beet root and chop into small pieces. Wash the greens. Add the coconut water and the lime juice to a blender. Add the beets and leaves along with a few cubes of ice. Blend well. Pour into a highball glass. Garnish with lime zest grated on the top of the drink.

TROPICAL CREAM

INGREDIENTS

25 ml melon syrup

25 ml freshly squeezed
  orange juice

25 ml double cream

20 ml coconut water

15 ml peach cordial

15 ml hazelnut syrup

Pineapple wedge and leaf,
  to garnish

ADD A TWIST

Try adding a spiced rum
for a deeply delicious
nutty edge.

A smooth and creamy, fruity cocktail with a
velvety texture. When you start a drink with
dark green melon syrup, you know that the
finished product is going to be fruity, tropical
and sweet.

METHOD

Add all of the ingredients to an ice-filled
cocktail shaker. Shake well. Strain into a
highball glass half full of crushed ice. Garnish
with a pineapple wedge on the rim of the glass
and float a leaf on top of the drink.

COCODA

INGREDIENTS

½ cantaloupe

20 ml coconut syrup

45 ml freshly pressed
   pineapple juice

25 ml cream

25 ml milk

Pineapple leaf and wedge
   and maraschino cherry,
   to garnish

ADD A TWIST

As with most tropical
drinks, this could benefit
from a shot of rum.

This drink is based on a Samoan dessert that
is made with coconut milk.

The cantaloupe, also known as the musk or
rock melon, is one of around twenty-five
varieties of melon. Its juicy flesh is orange-
coloured and sweet, and the seeds are relatively
easy to remove. Melon is a fruit with numerous
health-boosting properties. It's a wonderful
source of beta-carotene, which is most
commonly found in orange and yellow fruit.

METHOD

Cut the skin off the cantaloupe and put the
flesh into a blender along with the rest of the
ingredients, and a handful of ice. Blend for 30
seconds. Pour into a highball glass. Float a
pineapple leaf on the top of the drink and, for
added flair, garnish with a pineapple wedge
and a maraschino cherry on the rim.

KIWI KOOLER

INGREDIENTS

150 ml still water, chilled

2 sweet apples

½ avocado

3 kiwis

Handful of spinach

Apple wedge, to garnish

Kiwis may be small but they sure pack a punch: they're densely packed with vitamins and nutrients, fibre and protein. Also known as the Chinese Gooseberry, with its bright green colour and black seeds, it certainly brings a bit of drama to a drink.

METHOD

Put the water into the blender. Core and cut the apples into quarters. Peel the avocado and remove its stone. Peel and halve the kiwis. Blend everything together along with the spinach and a handful of ice. Pour into a highball glass. Garnish with a wedge of apple on the rim of the glass.

GREEN LIGHT

INGREDIENTS

1 ripe banana

1 large, ripe Hass avocado

30g plain zero-fat yogurt

100g cooked spinach,
    cooled and squeezed dry

2 tablespoons of agave
    syrup

Handful fresh parsley

Banana slice and cubes of
    avocado to garnish

For this recipe, the spinach needs to be boiled or steamed, so plan your preparations in advance. The cooking water will be packed with nutrients – you may want to let the liquid cool, store it, and include in your next smoothie! Or fill an ice cube container to use in cooking.

METHOD

Peel and slice the banana. Peel the avocado, remove the stone, and roughly chop the flesh. Blend all of the ingredients together, adding ice cubes until the mixture reaches your desired texture and consistency. Place a slice of banana and a cube of avocado on a toothpick or skewer. Drizzle both with a few drops of the agave syrup and place the decorated toothpick along the rim of the glass.

RISE AND SHINE

INGREDIENTS

30ml still water

60g spinach leaves

1 mango

Juice from 1 large orange

2 teaspoons flaxseed

2 teaspoons cashew nuts

Sliced orange for garnish

It's fair to say that these recipe ingredients look more like a list of items for a breakfast bowl than for a drink. Flaxseed is commonly known as linseed and comes in a golden yellow color or a softer darker version. Both add little in the way of taste but they do bring texture, fibre, and omega-3. Flaxseed is also a great source of calcium, vital for developing and maintaining teeth and bones.

METHOD

Put the water in a blender. Wash the spinach leaves. Peel the mango and chop into chunks. Squeeze the juice from the orange. Add to the blender along with the mango, spinach, seeds, nuts, and a handful of ice. Add more water if the consistency isn't to your liking. Garnish with an orange slice on the rim of the glass.

6 BERRIES

BLOOD & SAND

4 blood oranges
50 ml cranberry juice
25 ml peach cordial
Juice from wedge of lime
½ slice of blood orange and
   wedge of lime, to garnish

ADD A TWIST

To make this a traditional
Blood & Sand, add
scotch whisky.

This is a take on the 1980s classic Sex on the Beach (of which there are many variants.)

Blood oranges' colouring is due to an extra pigment. There are three varieties, of which the Moro is more commonly found in the U.S. They are stronger in taste than regular oranges and the skin is usually pitted as opposed to the smooth skin you see on regular oranges.

METHOD

Use the citrus juicer to extract the lovely deep red juice from the blood oranges. Strain the liquid into an ice-filled cocktail shaker. Add the cranberry juice, peach cordial and a squeeze of fresh lime juice. Shake well. Strain into an ice-filled Casablanca glass. Drop hlalf a slice of blood orange and a wedge of lime into the drink. The green, orange and red together create a vivid palette of colours and make for a rather dramatic-looking drink.

CRANBERRY CRUSH

75 ml orange juice

75 ml cranberry juice

20 ml ginger ale

Slice of orange, to garnish

ADD A TWIST

Gin or vodka are great choices for ginger and cranberry-based drinks.

This is one of my favourite drinks due to both its simplicity and taste – the dry cranberry and sweet orange combine well with the sparkle and length of ginger ale. I came across it in the 1990s and it's stayed with me. Takes seconds to make and goes down well with all ages and at all manner of functions. It also has a few variants: top with lemonade for a sweeter taste, ginger beer for a sharper finish, or sparkling water when you want the focus to be on the juice. I prefer freshly squeezed orange juice to store-bought, though it adds to the prep time.

METHOD

Pour the orange and cranberry juices into an ice-filled cocktail shaker. Shake until the juices have created a nice frothy head, then strain. Pour into a highball glass three-quarters full of ice. Add the ginger ale. Garnish with a slice of orange on the rim of the glass.

WOO WOO

INGREDIENTS

150 ml cranberry juice
20 ml peach cordial
Juice from lime wedge
Lime wedge, to garnish

ADD A TWIST

The Woo Woo is traditionally a vodka-based drink. Try experimenting with different flavoured vodkas for an extra twist!

Given its popularity as an alcoholic cocktail, this recipe, consisting largely of cranberry juice, shows off its efficacy as an alcohol-free counterpart. Laced with peach, the fruity, dry cranberry gets an added kick with a squeeze of fresh lime. The dry-sweet-sharp combo comes up trumps. It's the easiest recipe in the book and one of my long-standing favourites.

METHOD

Fill a highball glass with large ice cubes. Add the cranberry juice and stir in the peach cordial. Take a wedge of lime, give it a squeeze and drop the spent wedge into the drink. Give everything another stir, add a straw and serve.

C BREEZE

INGREDIENTS

75 ml grapefruit juice

75 ml cranberry juice

25 ml sparkling water/
   lemonade (see page 87)

2 x ½ slices of lemon,
   to garnish

ADD A TWIST

The cocktail version of this drink has vodka as its base; I suggest an orange or mandarin vodka to add interest here.

Is C for 'vitamin C' or 'cranberry?' In my book, it's for 'calm'. The Sea Breeze, a vodka-based cocktail, has its alcohol replaced with an innocent yet sparkling topping. It's plain sailing.

There are several drinks that fall into 'families' of cocktails, each requiring the same basic formulaic approach. The Breeze family, which also includes Iced Teas, Rickeys and Slings, is made up of cocktails with two fruit juices that create a new flavour as well as a new shade of drink. Here, the dryness of the cranberry mellows the tart grapefruit, while the finger of sparkling water imparts some zing.

METHOD

Fill a cocktail shaker three quarters full of ice. Add equal amounts of grapefruit juice and cranberry juice. Shake well. Strain into an ice-filled highball glass. Top with sparkling water or lemonade, depending on your taste preference. Garnish with the slices of lemon on the rim of the glass.

CRANTASTIC

INGREDIENTS

150 ml cranberry juice
45 ml apple juice
½ fresh lime
15 ml elderflower cordial
Club soda
Cranberries and lime
    wedge, to garnish

ADD A TWIST

Make this into a twist
on the classic Crantini
by adding a shot of
vodka, or take it one step
further and swap the
soda with prosecco for
a boozier version!

The dryness of the cranberry, the sweetness of
the apple and the citrus hit of lime, combined
with the fragrant elderflower, makes this easy
to drink and easy to make.

METHOD

Add all the ingredients, except the club soda,
to an ice-filled shaker. Shake well. Strain into
a highball glass three-quarters full of ice. Top
with club soda. Garnish with cranberries and
wedge of lime.

COSMOPOLITAN

INGREDIENTS

35 ml cranberry juice
10 ml fresh lime juice
1 teaspoon orange cordial
1 teaspoon lime cordial
Orange peel, to garnish

ADD A TWIST

The alcoholic version found in bars across the globe contains a jigger of citron vodka.

Commonly known as the Cosmo, this classic contemporary cocktail was popularized in the 1990s and gained street cred as the drink of choice for *Sex and the City*'s fictional Carrie Bradshaw and friends Samantha, Charlotte and Miranda.

METHOD

Fill a martini glass with crushed ice. While the glass is chilling, add all the ingredients to a cocktail shaker filled with ice. Shake well. Remove the ice from the martini glass – it should be nicely frosted. Strain the drink into the martini glass. Now for the dramatic effect!

Cut a round 'coin' of orange peel, at least 2.5 centimetres in diameter, and hold between your thumb and forefinger. Use a cigarette lighter or light a match with your other hand, and hold the flame above the orange peel. Twist and squeeze the peel over the flame to release the orange's essential oils. Drop the peel into the drink to impart a slightly burnt yet enticing orange taste. This garnish is just as much about the flair as it is about the flavour.

ROSEBERRY LEMON COOLER

INGREDIENTS

2 tablespoons simple syrup

Sprig of fresh rosemary

50ml cranberry juice

Juice from lemon wedge

Soda water

Sprig of rosemary and
  lemon slice for garnish

Earthy rosemary, fresh lemon, and dry cranberry form a terrific trio of flavours.

Note: This infusion will also need to be prepared well in advance of serving.

METHOD

Put the simple syrup in a pan that's already on low heat. Add the sprig of rosemary; the warmth of the syrup will release the oils and tease the flavors out of the herb. Take the pan off the heat and let the rosemary steep for an hour. Remove the rosemary and chill the mixture. Add the syrup to an ice-filled cocktail shaker. Add the cranberry and lemon juices. Shake well. Strain into a Casablanca glass with large ice cubes in it. Top with soda water. Garnish with a lemon slice on the rim of the glass and a sprig of rosemary.

APRICOT APPETIZER

INGREDIENTS

2 apricots
100g fresh strawberries
100ml freshly squeezed
   orange juice
50ml sparkling water
Orange slice and
   strawberry for garnish

Apricots have been cultivated since antiquity, and dried ones were an important commodity on Persian trade routes. Sweet and fragrant, golden-orange apricots remain an important fruit in modern-day Iran where they are known under the common name of Zard-ālū. The Greeks were the first to bring them to Europe and called them the "golden eggs of the sun."

Because the skin is edible and tasty, it's possible to make this drink with the skin washed and left on. It comes down to the texture of the drink and the power of your blender; a lot of the modern, more compact, blenders have an extremely powerful action that blitzes everything (within reason) that you put into it. If your machine isn't one of these types then you may not want to serve this drink with little bits of skin in it that haven't been totally pulverized.

METHOD

Remove the apricot stones. Rinse, hull, and slice the strawberries. Blend all of the fruit and orange juice together along with a scoop of crushed ice. Pour into a highball glass. Top with a little sparkling water before giving the drink a final stir. Garnish.

RASPBERRY RAZZLE

INGREDIENTS

12 fresh raspberries

1 scoop vanilla ice cream

20 ml double cream

45 ml raspberry cordial

10 ml lime cordial

2 fresh raspberries,
   to garnish

ADD A TWIST

The slightly sour fruitiness of the raspberry would be nicely complemented by the addition of vanilla vodka.

Sharp and sweet at the same time, this drink makes for a fabulous dessert.

METHOD

Wash the raspberries. Blend together with the vanilla ice cream, double cream, the raspberry and lime cordials and a scoop of ice. Pour into a Casblanca glass. Float two raspberries on the top of the drink.

LETTUCE EAT BERRIES

Juice from 2 large oranges
4 large strawberries
Handful frozen blueberries
2 teaspoons chia seeds
½ head of iceberg lettuce
70g low-fat plain yogurt
Orange slice for garnish

Smoothies can be a great way of cleaning out the fridge and putting to good use leftover salads, fruits, and vegetables. Even putting a small amount of each in the compost bin can feel like a waste of money. Rather than throwing out leftover iceberg lettuce, I threw it in this mix instead. I've been so pleased with the end result, I've taken to saving lettuce just to make this drink.

Note: Frozen blueberries go in this mix so we don't need ice.

METHOD

Squeeze the oranges and pour the fresh juice into the blender. Blend with the rest of the ingredients. Pour into a highball glass. Garnish with an orange wheel on the rim of the glass.

FRUIT SPIRAL

100g iceberg lettuce

3 fresh large strawberries

150ml soy milk

2 teaspoons of spirulina

1 banana

Sliced strawberry for
  garnish

Spirulina is a natural algae powder packed with antioxidants, protein, vitamins A, B, and C, and iron.

METHOD

Wash and chop the lettuce and strawberries. Blend along with the soy milk, spirulina, banana, and a handful of ice. Pour into a highball glass. Garnish with a slice of strawberry.

BERRY BLAST

INGREDIENTS

6 fresh raspberries
6 fresh strawberries
6 fresh blueberries
6 fresh blackberries
25 ml elderflower cordial
Juice from 1 lime
10 ml sugar syrup
Ginger beer
Fresh berries and metal
    cocktail stick, to garnish

ADD A TWIST

Lemon-flavoured vodka
would transform this
into a spin-off on
berry lemonade.

One of the most popular cocktails in the world, the Mojito, requires a muddler to gently bruise the mint and coax out the flavours from the leaves. With this drink, there's no coaxing of flavours per se but, instead, a barbaric bashing of berries to turn them into a fabulously fresh purée. The aroma is wonderful and hints at the drink that is to come.

Note: take care to point the shaker away from you when making this drink, so you don't end up with stained clothes from errant berry juices.

METHOD

Muddle the berries in the base of a cocktail shaker. Squeeze in the fresh lime juice. Add the sugar syrup, cordial and a handful of ice cubes. Shake well. Strain into handled jars filled with crushed ice. Top with ginger beer. Spear extra berries on a metal cocktail pick and lay across the top of the glass to garnish.

KALE & STRAWBERRY SMOOTHIE

INGREDIENTS

100g kale

6 fresh large strawberries

50g low-fat plain yogurt

2 tablespoons skim milk

2 teaspoons runny honey
(or to taste)

Thinly sliced strawberry
for garnish

Frozen fruits can be just as good for you as the non-frozen variety. The fruits' nutrients have been locked in not long after the fruit has been picked. Most fresh fruit withstands lots of travel time and has been sitting on the shelf before making its way into your kitchen. Stock up on frozen fruits. They have the added benefit of providing the ice factor if you run out of cubes.

METHOD

Blend the kale and strawberries, along with the yogurt, milk, and a handful of ice. Add the honey to taste. Garnish with strawberry slices on the top of the drink and eat them as you drink.

BERRY NICE

INGREDIENTS

Handful fresh raspberries
50ml still water, chilled
50ml orange juice
20ml raspberry cordial
1 teaspoon light cream
1 teaspoon simple syrup
1 raspberry for garnish

This drink can double as dessert.

Apart from the usual red and purple raspberries, they can also be found in black and gold, the gold ones being exceptionally sweet.

METHOD

Add a handful of ice to a martini glass and leave it to chill while you prepare the drink. Blend the raspberries with water for 10 seconds. Pour the fresh raspberry liquid into an ice-filled cocktail shaker along with the other ingredients. Shake well. Strain into the chilled martini glass. Garnish with a raspberry dropped into the drink.

FRUITS OF THE FOREST

INGREDIENTS

10 fresh blackberries

10 fresh raspberries

15 ml blackberry cordial

15 ml raspberry cordial

75 ml cranberry juice

25 ml still water

Juice of 1 lime

Club soda

1 blackberry and
    1 raspberry, to garnish

ADD A TWIST

Pimm's No. 1 liqueur
would be a lovely addition
to this drink.

For many of us, childhood memories entail
picking blackberries and raspberries and making
jams, jellies or pies with them. Reminisce and
relive those days with this fresh and fruity berry
delight. Both berries are rich in vitamins C and
K and omega-3, and help to give this drink a
healthy kick.

METHOD

Muddle the berries in the base of a cocktail
shaker. Add the cordials, cranberry juice, water,
lime juice and a generous handful of ice. Shake
well. Strain into a highball glass half full of ice.
Top with club soda. Float the raspberry and
blackberry on the top of the drink.

STRAWBERRY MULE

INGREDIENTS

Piece of fresh ginger

Slice of fresh red chilli
pepper (seeds removed)

1 teaspoon sugar syrup

20 ml fresh
strawberry purée

Juice of ½ lime

Ginger beer

Lime wedge and strawberry,
to garnish

ADD A TWIST

If you dare, add even
more spice with a slug of
spiced rum.

Our take on the ubiquitous Moscow Mule, which derives its name from the 'kick' of the ginger beer and the city of Moscow, since Russia was long associated with vodka. Fresh strawberry and lime sweetens the drink, adds some colour and vibrancy, and counterbalances the heat. Experiment with the amount of chilli and ginger you use. Personally, I use more than what's listed; I love the invasion of heat after the initial sweet and fizzy combo of the strawberry-ginger.

With sweet and sour, fire and ice, and red and green, this is another drink that will draw ooohs and aaahs from your guests.

METHOD

Using a muddler or the flat disc end of a bar spoon, muddle together a thumb-sized piece of fresh ginger with a one-inch slice of chilli, and sugar syrup in the base of a cocktail shaker. Add the strawberry purée, the lime juice and a good scoop of ice. Shake all the ingredients together and double strain into an ice-filled highball glass. Top with the ginger beer. Garnish with a lime wedge and strawberry on the rim of the glass.

SUMMER RAIN

75 g fresh strawberries
Juice from 5 large oranges
45 ml lemonade
Juice from 2 lime wedges
Lime wedge and strawberry,
   to garnish

ADD A TWIST

Add a measure of
vodka to turn this into
a Summer Storm.

Packed with the taste of summer and given length and sparkle by the addition of lemonade, this drink is as colourful as it is fresh and vibrant.

In many of these recipes the question of fresh juice versus concentrate is open to interpretation and personal preference. Here, however, the orange juice needs to be freshly squeezed.

The berries and the citrus are all prepared from scratch, so this drink is as fresh as can be. Strawberries are packed full of health-boosting vitamins C and K as well as antioxidants.

METHOD

Rinse, hull and slice the strawberries. Squeeze the juice of 5 large oranges and blend along with the strawberries and a handful of crushed ice. Pour into a highball glass with a few ice cubes. Top with the lemonade and the juice from two lime wedges. Drop the spent wedges into the drink. Perch a lime wedge on the rim of the glass along with a fresh strawberry.

BLUEBERRY & GINGER CUP

INGREDIENTS

Handful of blueberries

10 ml fresh lemon juice

15 ml vanilla extract

10 ml sugar syrup (see
  page 27)

10 ml fresh ginger juice

75 ml cranberry juice

Blueberries, ½ slice of
  lemon and ½ slice of lime,
  to garnish

Made with fresh blueberries, lemon juice, ginger and cranberry, this drink is a pleasant assault on the senses. The fresh berries and citrus give a lovely aroma; the drink itself is a beautiful, deep red colour with a garnish of yellow and blue; the ice provides a satisfying crunch; and the taste is wonderful.

Blueberries are a known source of vitamins C and K and provide the body with a good supply of antioxidants, benefitting the brain and the nervous system. Scientific research proves that blueberries not only help improve memory function, but they also slow the onset of problems associated with aging.

METHOD

Place the blueberries in the base of a cocktail shaker and add the lemon juice. Muddle together. Add the vanilla, sugar syrup, ginger juice and a large scoop of ice. Shake well. Fill a Casablanca glass two-thirds with crushed ice. Strain into the glass. Add the cranberry juice. Stir well. Top with more crushed ice. Drop a few blueberries and the lemon and lime slices into the drink.

NUTTY GOJI MARTINI

INGREDIENTS

150 ml goji berry juice
20 ml orgeat
Sparkling water
Lime wedge, to garnish

ADD A TWIST

Pair the orgeat, which is
used in many tropical
drinks, with rum for an
even more tropical flavour.

Dried goji berries look and taste like, and can
be used in the same way as, dried cranberries.
They've been grown, cultivated, eaten and drunk
in the Himalayas and China for centuries. There
are vastly exaggerated claims but what is not
disputed is that the iron-rich berries *do* contain
beneficial vitamins and nutrients like zinc,
potassium, selenium, and vitamins A
and C.

METHOD

Pour the goji berry juice into an ice-filled
shaker. Add the orgeat. Shake well. Strain into
an ice-filled Casablanca glass. Top with
sparkling water. Garnish with a wedge of lime
on the rim of the glass.

AÇAI & MELON MARTINI

INGREDIENTS

2 large slices watermelon
75 ml açai berry juice
25 ml freshly pressed
    apple juice
15 ml fresh lime juice
Apple and watermelon
    slices, to garnish

ADD A TWIST

A slug of golden rum
would add a little caramel
sweetness to these lovely
tropical flavours.

When the açai berry moved out of the Brazilian rainforest and into the city, largely due to surfers and sporting aficionados who extolled the berry's many virtues and gulped down the fruit on a daily basis, the world of food science took note. The popularity of the açai berry is due to its amino acids, which help muscles perform and aid endurance and stamina. These purple berries are also rich in antioxidants, essential fatty acids, and vitamins A, B, and E, and are a great source of magnesium, zinc, copper, and calcium. No wonder the açai berry has been elevated to the status of superfood.

METHOD

Cut away the flesh from the skin of the watermelon and remove as many of the seeds as possible. Muddle the watermelon in the base of a cocktail shaker. Add the açai berry juice, apple juice and the freshly squeezed lime. Fill with ice cubes. Shake well. Double strain into a chilled martini glass. Garnish with apple and watermelon slices on the side of the glass.

BLUEBERRY MUFFIN

INGREDIENTS

Handful of blueberries

10 ml fresh lemon juice

15 ml vanilla extract

10 ml sugar syrup

10 ml gingerbread syrup
(see page 32)

75 ml cranberry juice

Blueberries and slice of
lemon, to garnish

ADD A TWIST

Bourbon or whisky
would add a nice caramel
flavour, making this
cocktail taste even more
like a blueberry muffin.

This is a delicious after-dinner drink or perfect as part of an indulgent afternoon tea.

Blueberries are an excellent source of vitamins C and K and useful antioxidants, which benefit the brain and the nervous system.

METHOD

Place the blueberries in the base of a cocktail shaker and add the lemon juice. Muddle together. Add the vanilla, sugar syrup, gingerbread syrup and a large scoop of ice. Shake well. Fill a Casablanca glass two-thirds with crushed ice. Strain into the glass. Add the cranberry juice. Stir well. Top with more crushed ice. Add two straws. Spear blueberries on a metal cocktail pick and lay across the top of the glass. Add the slice of lemon to the rim of the glass.

AÇAI BREEZE

INGREDIENTS

75 ml cranberry juice
75 ml açai berry juice
45 ml apple juice
Lemon slices, to garnish

ADD A TWIST

If you want to add
alcohol to this drink, vodka
would be the natural
choice to offset the
powerful berry flavours.

These purple berries look like grapes and often taste like red wine. Because of its many virtues, the açai berry is often marketed as an 'ultra premium superfood'. A plentiful source of iron, the berries also contain vitamins A, B1, B2, B3 and E, as well as fatty and amino acids, and antioxidant-rich – good for body, mind and soul.

Note: for this recipe, it's important to use large ice cubes as they take longer to melt.

METHOD

Fill a highball glass with large ice cubes. Stir all the ingredients together well, then add more ice if it has reduced in size. Garnish with a couple of lemon slices dropped into the drink.

LINGER ON

INGREDIENTS

100ml lingonberry juice
100ml grapefruit juice
Juice from lime wedge
Ginger ale
Lime slice for garnish

Lingonberries – the Scandinavian equivalent of blackberries – are a smaller cousin of the cranberry. Indeed, they are known as mountain cranberries and partridge berries in the parts of North America where they can be found.

It's a quite bitter and sour fruit, so with this cocktail also containing grapefruit juice and fresh lime, you can see where we'll end up with the overall taste. Sharp and with quite a kick, this is a real pick-me-up.

METHOD

Pour the juices into an ice-filled shaker. Shake well. Strain into an ice-filled highball glass. Top with ginger ale. Garnish with a lime slice on the rim of the glass.

7 BEANS

COCOA

COFFEE

CHOC ORANGE SPICE

75 ml whole milk

1 cinnamon stick

10 ml freshly squeezed
    orange juice

15 ml chocolate syrup
    (see page 32)

25 ml double cream

Grated nutmeg and cocoa
    powder, to garnish

ADD A TWIST

The injection of a smoky
single malt whiskey to this
flavour combo would be
ideal here; we all know
how well chocolate and
whisky pair up together.

A drink for the chocaholics among us, complete
with chocolate syrup, cocoa powder, and
sprinkles! The type of milk you use – whole,
low-fat, skim or fat-free – is dependent on your
own taste and preference. For this particular
recipe, however, I recommend using whole milk
for extra creaminess.

METHOD

Slowly heat the milk in a small pan with the
cinnamon stick. Gently simmer for 2 to 3
minutes to bring out the spice of the cinnamon
stick. Leave to cool, then remove the cinnamon
stick. Add the spiced milk to an ice-filled
cocktail shaker along with the orange juice,
chocolate syrup and double cream. Shake well.
Fill an old-fashioned glass halfway with crushed
ice. Strain into the glass. Garnish with a pinch
of grated nutmeg and cocoa powder.

VIVA EL CHOCTEL!

INGREDIENTS

1 young coconut or 500 ml
   coconut milk
1 small red or green chilli
1.25 cm vanilla pod
1 cardamom seed
30–45 ml raw
   cacao powder
Sea or rock salt

ADD A TWIST

Add a shot of white creme
de cacao to up the ante on
the chocolate stakes.

The word 'Cocktail' in Spanish is 'Coctel', so I
introduced an 'H' into both words and created
a new word; wholly self-explanatory.

Make a creamy chocolate drink using the water
and flesh of a young coconut (or use coconut
milk if you prefer.) Raw cacao adds a chocolate
hit and chilli, cardamom and salt combine to
lift the whole thing into something really special.

METHOD

If using a fresh coconut, cut it open, catching
all the milk. Scrape out the flesh. Put the flesh
and milk (or coconut milk, if using) into a
blender. Cut open the chilli, scrape out and
discard the seeds. Crush lightly with the back
of a knife and add as much as you like to the
blender (you can always add more at the end.)
Cut open and crush the vanilla pod and add to
the blender. Bash the cardamom seed with a
wooden spoon to release the oils. Put the
cardamom seed and cacao powder into the
blender and whiz everything for a minute until
smooth. Add a little salt to taste. Pour into a
highball glass to serve.

BANOFFEE & PASSION SHAKE

INGREDIENTS

3 pieces dark chocolate

3 pieces milk chocolate

1 fresh vanilla pod

75 ml milk

1 dessert spoon
  caster sugar

25 ml toffee sauce

10 ml banana syrup

10 ml butterscotch syrup

25 ml single cream

1 fresh passion fruit

Banana slice, to garnish

ADD A TWIST

For a low-alcohol addition to this drink, introduce a measure of passion fruit liqueur to the shaker.

Passion fruit adds a delicious tartness to this interesting cocktail, which perfectly counteracts some of the sweetness of the other ingredients. Its flesh and seeds also make it uniquely pretty.

METHOD

Place the chocolate in a small heatproof bowl. Bring about an inch of water to simmer in a saucepan or pot. Set the bowl in the mouth of the pot, making sure the water doesn't touch the bottom of the bowl. Stir the chocolate as it melts. Carefully coat the inside of the martini glass with the melted chocolate for a marbled effect. Chill the glass.

Make the vanilla milk: split the vanilla pod, remove its seeds and add both to a small milk pan. Slowly heat the milk to boiling. Remove from heat and leave to cool. Strain out the pod and seeds. Halve the passion fruit and scoop out the flesh. Pour the vanilla milk along with the rest of the ingredients into an ice-filled cocktail shaker. Shake well. Strain into the chocolate-decorated martini glass. Garnish with a banana slice on the rim.

ESPRESSO MARTINI

INGREDIENTS

125–150 ml cold
   espresso coffee
25 ml caramel syrup
15 ml sugar syrup (or
   to taste)
3 coffee beans, to garnish

ADD A TWIST

Try this with an espresso-
flavoured vodka for an
even richer coffee taste.

This Espresso Martini is a take on the vodka-based contemporary classic. With its handsome, creamy foam top and its dark-brown body, this two-toned, caffeine-fuelled cocktail is the perfect after-dinner drink. While it can be made with instant coffee, it's best to use freshly ground coffee beans. For the ultimate pick-me-up, serve this as shots.

METHOD

Pour 300 millilitres of boiling water into a French Press containing 2 teaspoons of coffee (instant or freshly ground). Stir and leave for 5 minutes. Stir again, then plunge, and leave for another 5 minutes before pouring the coffee into a mug. Leave to cool.

Put the cold coffee into an ice-filled cocktail shaker. Add the caramel syrup and the sugar syrup to taste. Shake well. Strain into a chilled martini glass. To garnish, float three coffee beans on the top of the drink.

NUTS ABOUT COFFEE

25 ml whole milk

25 ml double cream

35 ml strong cold espresso
coffee

10 ml caramel syrup

15 ml orgeat

Grated chocolate,
to garnish

ADD A TWIST

Whisky or rum would add
extra depth of flavour to
this martini.

The nuts in this case are almonds; the almond
flavour itself is contained in the syrup that goes
by the name orgeat. For the taste profile of this
drink to work, the coffee needs to be strong,
hence the use of espresso. You may choose to
use a little less caramel syrup as the orgeat is
also quite sweet.

METHOD

Fill a martini glass with crushed ice to chill it.
While it's chilling, add all of the ingredients to
an ice-filled cocktail shaker. Shake well. Remove
the ice from the martini glass; it should be
nicely frosted. Fine-strain into a martini glass.
Garnish with chocolate (white, dark, or milk
– your choice) grated over top.

8 PITCHER PARTY

PREP AND PRE-PARTY PLANNING

Let's say you have six to eight dinner guests and will have an hour of drinks before food is served. Practice making your drink from start to finish. You need to know how long it takes you to make one before you set about making a number of them for several (waiting) guests. This is also an excellent way to be certain you have all the right equipment, ingredients, glassware and garnishes. Think of it as your trial run. Glasses, too, can be garnished in advance, so you have an effortless transition from one style of drink to the next.

If you're setting out a number of drinks on a bar surface or table, to greet guests as they arrive, arrange them in a circle or other shape. If the occasion is to honour an individual or a couple, how about laying the glasses out to form their initial(s)?

So now you know what you're making, how you're going to embellish and present it, now you just need to know how many people you are making each drink for. Most recipes are for one person, though I have included a few punches in the chapter that are good for groups.

Enjoy shaking, stirring and blending your way through this collection of fun, colourful and tasty alcohol-free cocktails. Cheers and good health!

CHOOSING RECIPES

Don't give your guests anything too outlandish. Something not too sharp or too sweet is a good starting point. Remember: first impressions matter. Choose a recipe heavy on the 'wow' factor: it should look as good as it tastes. A garnish of bright strawberry red and deep lime green provide a nice stark contrast. Make sure there's enough fresh ice in the drinks. Be sure to stir the drinks as you hand them out. Everyone likes the refreshing sound of ice clinking against the side of the glass. It also signals the amount of care you've put into every aspect of composing the drink – from choosing the freshest ingredients to making sure its taste hasn't been watered down. Before your first guest has even taken a sip, you will have already appealed to four of the five senses: the colourful garnish elicits the sense of sight; the smell of fresh fruit hanging in the air teases the nose; the clinking of the ice perks up the ears; and the refreshingly cold glass pleasantly sparks the sensation of touch.

If you'll need to serve another drink and want to vary things a little, a punch is good for the next offering as you can have the whole bowl or pitcher already made up, leaving only ice to be added at the last minute.

Dairy drinks are often a suitable accompaniment to desserts, whereas the sharpness of a citrusy drink makes a great aperitif. It goes without saying that non-alcoholic versions of classics make for the ideal party beverage. Although most ingredients are available online (or in today's well-stocked supermarkets) year-round, there are still foods and flavours we associate with certain times of year, so do try using 'seasonal' ingredients.

PRETTY AS A PITCHER

SERVES 6

INGREDIENTS

200 ml raspberries

150 ml pear juice

Juice from 3 limes

1 litre ginger beer

Handful of raspberries and
    lime slices, to garnish

ADD A TWIST

Vodka or gin work nicely
with the fruit flavours here.

As its name suggests, this is a drink to be prepared and served by the pitcher.

Technically, raspberries aren't fruit but, instead, come from the rose family, of which there are over two hundred varieties. High in fibre and low in calories, raspberries contain more vitamin C than oranges.

METHOD

Wash the raspberries and blend with the pear juice. Fill a pitcher half full of crushed ice. Add the lime juice. Pour the blended raspberry and pear mix into the pitcher. Top with ginger beer and drop whole raspberries into the drink. Make sure everyone gets at least one raspberry in their ice-filled glass. Garnish with lime slices on the rim of each glass.

LEMON REFRESHER

INGREDIENTS

800 g sugar

200 ml fresh mint leaves

½ litre of fresh lemon juice

2 litres of soda water

4 fresh limes

Sprig of mint and slices
  of lemon, to garnish

This fabulous summer punch is ideally served in a glass punchbowl to show off its vivid greens and yellows.

This requires a bit of pre-prep for the mint-infused sugar syrup. Best to plan in advance.

METHOD

Boil a kettle full of water and put a heavy-based pan on the heat. Pour the boiling water into the pan. Add the sugar; it will take only a minute or two for the sugar to dissolve completely. Turn off the heat to let cool. Once the mixture is at room temperature, add the mint leaves and stir well into the sugar-water. Leave overnight to infuse.

The next day, put a dozen ice cubes into a punchbowl. Add the lemon juice, and pour in the sugar-water. Top with soda. Chop four limes into quarters and squeeze the juice into the punch. Ladle into ice-filled handled jars. Garnish each drink with a sprig of mint and a slice of lemon.

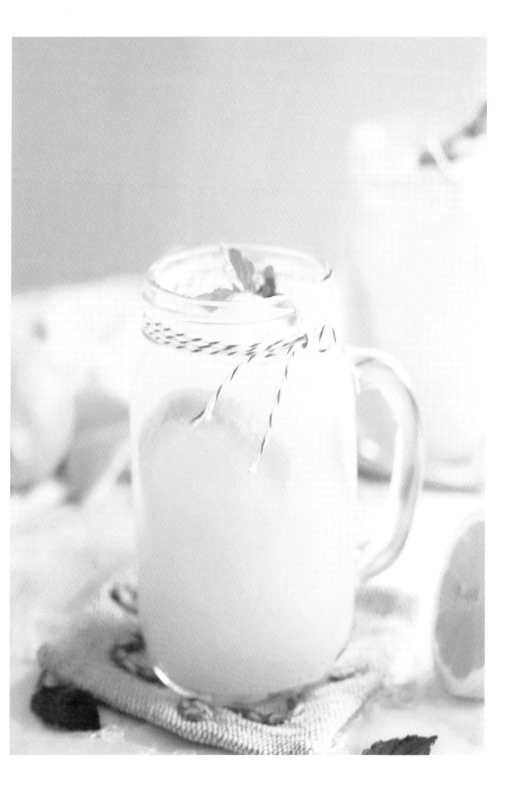

WATERMELON & BASIL COOLER

SERVES 6

INGREDIENTS

20 large fresh basil leaves,
    plus 6 to garnish
1 watermelon
150 ml still water, chilled
Juice from 1 lime
6 slices of lime, to garnish

The hardest part about making this drink is preparing the watermelon; it requires some effort to cut it into smaller pieces for blending. The best part of this drink may be its aroma of fresh lime and basil. A summer mix like this begs to be served alongside a picnic of sandwiches and fresh fruits.

METHOD

Place the basil leaves in a large glass jug. Carve the watermelon into boats first and then carve out the sections. Cut thinly so you can pop out the seeds with the point of a knife. Don't worry if you can't extract all of the seeds. Do your best to preserve as much of the fruit's flesh as possible.

Blend the watermelon with the water, lime juice and a few ice cubes. Pour into a large glass jug. Muddle the basil leaves against the inside of the jug. Stir well. Pour into highball glasses filled with crushed ice. Stick the left-over basil leaves into the lime slices and garnish.

FRUIT TEA REFRESHER

SERVES 4

INGREDIENTS

---

2 herbal fruit tea bags of
    your choice
600 ml cold water
1 cinnamon stick
1 vanilla pod
Grated orange zest
5 tellicherry peppercorns
15 ml ginger cordial
25 ml fresh lemon juice
10 ml sugar syrup
1 raspberry; 1 sprig of mint;
    and 1 piece of fresh
    ginger, to garnish

Best made as a large batch due to the amount of work that goes into the making. Even though you're making a large batch, serve and garnish each drink separately, as the garnishes add a fair bit to the overall drink.

You can vary the type of fruit tea used.

METHOD

Brew the tea. Add the cinnamon stick, vanilla pod, grated orange zest and tellicherry peppercorns to the teapot. Leave to cool and infuse. Strain the cold tea into an ice-filled cocktail shaker. Add the ginger cordial, lemon juice and sugar syrup. Shake well. Strain into an ice-filled Casablanca glass. Peel the skin off the ginger before placing it in the drink next to a sprig of mint and a raspberry perched on the edge of the glass.

SUMMER SANGRIA

INGREDIENTS

1 apple
1 lemon
1 lime
1 orange
1 peach
Handful of strawberries
½ litre red grape juice
100 ml orange juice
Sugar syrup, to taste
400 ml sparkling water
100 ml ginger beer

This drink's name comes from its colour: 'sangre' is Spanish for blood. Commonly made from red wine, this version uses grape juice instead.

This drink is best as a 'pitcher cocktail', ideal for casual parties. Guests help themselves to refills and everyone is free to socialize! Fruit garnishes make this an especially great summer drink. It's fresh, cool and colourful, and by altering the ratio of one or two ingredients, each pitcher can be slightly different than the last. Salud!

METHOD

You'll need at least three of the following: apple, lemon, lime, orange, peach or strawberry. Slice or chop the fruit into cubes or crescents. Combine red grape juice and orange juice in a 5:1 ratio and add sugar syrup to taste. (You can add more of the latter prior to serving.) Add the fruit and leave the mix in the fridge to soak for a few hours. Before serving, add plenty of ice and top with four parts sparkling water to one part ginger beer. If serving from a punchbowl, don't forget the ladle so guests can help themselves.

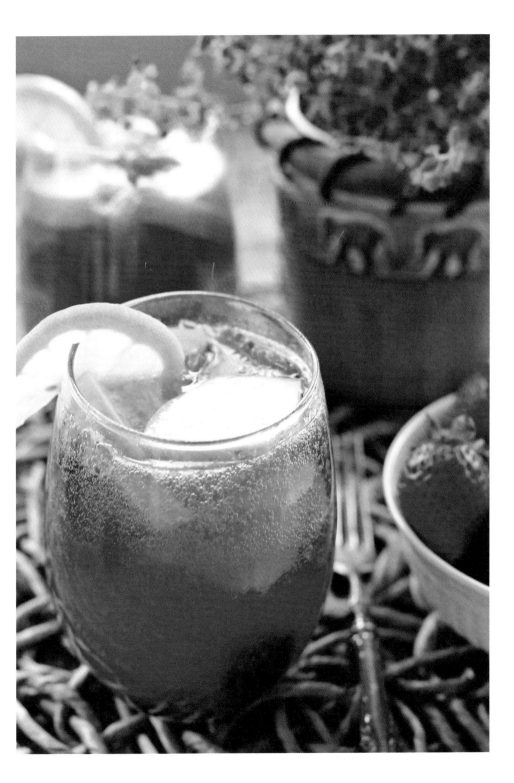

VIRGIN MARY

INGREDIENTS

½ teaspoon celery salt
½ teaspoon black pepper
480 ml fresh tomato juice
12 drops of Worcestershire
  sauce
8 drops of Tabasco
Juice of 2 lemons or limes
1 teaspoon of horseradish
4 celery sticks and 4 slices
  of lemon, to garnish

ADD A TWIST

The original version is
made with vodka, but
some also opt to make
their Bloody Mary with
gin, when the cocktail
becomes a Red Snapper.

Let me tell you a secret (though don't let the marketers, purveyors and distillers of vodka hear it): most vodkas impart little taste to a drink. It's colourless, flavourless and characterless and serves only to give its recipient a 'hit' of alcohol.

This drink was first made in Harry's New York Bar in 1920s Paris, and named for Queen Mary I. A great Virgin Mary needs as much attention to detail as a Bloody Mary.

METHOD

Put the celery salt in the base of a jug and add the black pepper. Half fill with good quality fresh tomato juice. Add the Worcestershire sauce, Tabasco, lemon or lime juice, horseradish and a handful of ice. Stir vigorously. Strain into four ice-filled highball glasses. Garnish each with a celery stick and slice of lemon.

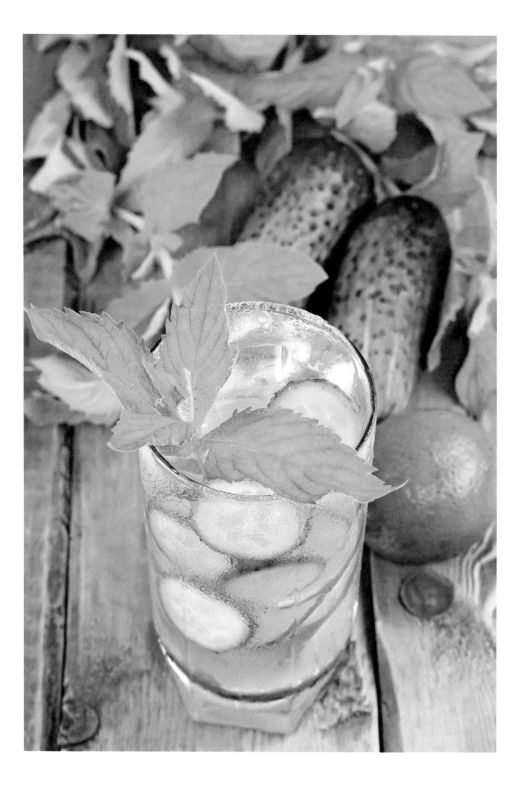

INDEX

Page references in italics indicate images

A
Açai Breeze 143
Açai & Melon Martini 140
agave syrup 54, 109
alcohol-free drinks 10-11
Amaretto 71
Angostura bitters 94
apple juice 40, 120, 140, 143
apples 46, 60, 106, 168
avocados 106, 109

B
Banoffee & Passion Shake 151
basil 42, 74, 164
Bee's Knees Martini 76, 77
Beet It! 103
Bellini, Citrus 78, *79*
Bermudan Breeze 102
Berry Blast 128, *129*
blackberries 128, 133
black currant syrup 100
blenders 20
blood orange juice 70
blood oranges 114
Blood & Sand 114, *115*
Bloody Mary 170, *171*
blueberries 126, 128, 136, 142
Blueberry & Ginger Cup 136, *137*
Blueberry Muffin 142
bourbon 11, 64, 142

Breakfast Boost 70
Brush with Basil, A 42, *43*
build method 25
butterscotch syrup 59, 151

C
C Breeze 118, *119*
Caipirinha 83
caramel syrup 59, 152, 154
cardamom 52, 53, 150
Cardamom Martini 53
Caribbean Float 98
celery 60, 170
chile 134, 150
Choc Orange Spice 148, *149*
chocolate 59, 150, 151, 154
  syrup 32, 148
cinnamon sticks 32, 39, 52, 148, 165
cinnamon syrup 32, 44
Citrus Bellini 78, *79*
cloves 39
club soda 39, 120, 133
Cocktail Thyme 47
Cocoda 105
coconut cream 92
coconut milk 48, 98, 102, 104, 150
coconut syrup 105
coconut water 62, 91, 102, 103, 104
coffee 154
Coriander & Cardamom Tonic 52
coriander seeds 39, 52
Cosmopolitan 121
Cranberry Crush 116

cranberry juice 42, 82, 114–22, 133, 136, 142, 143
Crantastic 120
cream 59, 104, 105, 124, 131, 148, 151, 154
cucumber 60, 90

D
Daiquiri, Lychee 100, *101*

E
Earl Grey Lemon Mar-Tea-Ni 56, *57*
Elder Statesman, The 39
Elderflower Collins 38
elderflower cordial 38-40, 120
Elderflower Fizz *36*, 37
elderflower liqueur 39
elderflower syrup 37
Espresso Martini 152, *153*

F
fruit cordials/juices/purées 28-29
Fruit Tea Refresher 165
Fruits of the Forest *132*, 133

G
garnish 33
gin 37, 38, 42, 47, 57, 58, 70, 74, 77, 82, 86, 94, 116, 160, 170
ginger 52, 54, 57, 58, 60, 134
  beer 70, 102, 116, 128, 134, 160, 168
cordial 165

Acknowledgements

Huge thanks to my wife, Catherine, and daughters, Emma and Phoebe, for their patience while recipes were tweaked, and for their willingness to give candid feedback on new drinks.

Picture credits

P. 2 Shutterstock by Ziashusha
Pp. 4–5 Getty Images by Rusty Hill
P. 9 Shutterstock
Pp. 12–13 Getty Images by Westend61
Pp. 18–19 Shutterstock by JurateBuiviene
P. 27 Getty Images by Alexandra Grablewski

P. 30 Shutterstock by Natalie Barth
P. 36 Getty Images by William Shaw
P. 43 Getty Images by The Picture Pantry
P. 55 Getty Images by Alexandra Grablewski
P. 61 by Joe Woodhouse
Pp. 72–73 Getty Images by Annabelle Breakey
P. 80 Shutterstock by Shustikova Inessa
Pp. 96–97 Shutterstock by Ziashusha
Pp. 166–167 Getty Images by Silke Zander/ Picture Press
P. 172 Shutterstock by Tatiana Volgutova

First published in Great Britain, Australia and New Zealand in 2019
by Modern Books
An imprint of Elwin Street Productions Limited
14 Clerkenwell Green
London EC1R 0DP
www.modern-books.com

ISBN 978-1-911130-64-2

10 9 8 7 6 5 4 3 2 1

Printed in China